SMALL BUSINESS STRATEGIC PLANNING

CREATING SUSTAINABLE SUCCESS

Build a Small Business Strategic Plan and Implement It!

Claudia J. Pannell

Joanne H. Osmond

Vision Tree Forums

This publication is designed to provide accurate and authoritative information in regard to the subject-matter covered. It is sold with the understanding that the publisher is not engaged in rendering legal, accounting, or other professional services. If legal advice or other expert assistance is required, the services of a competent professional should be sought.

Editorial Assistant: Barbara L. Coffing

Copyright © 2010 by Vision Tree Forums

Published by The Vision Tree, Ltd.
216 Waterbury Circle, Lake Villa, IL 60046
Jo@TheVisionTree.com
847.356.7550 Fax: 847.356.3783

Printed in the United States of America
ISBN: 978-1-933334-21-9

Acknowledgement

In the local community where we live and work, there are many small business owners and professionals who continue to amaze us with their hard work and their continuing support for others around them. Supporting all of us are the College of Lake County and the Illinois Small Business Development Center. Without them many small businesses would not have succeeded or kept their doors open. We thank the instructors, counselors, and leaders for the inspiration they provide our business community.

Table of Contents

Transform ~ Innovate ~ Stabilize ~ Grow

Operations Strategy

Strategic planning results in sustainable success. Writing a strategic plan for your organization is a journey that begins thoughtfully.

The outcomes for this chapter are outlined below. At the beginning of each chapter we use a chart format that is similar to the 1-PSP (One-Page Strategic Plan) which is a tool used in our strategic planning process.

Company →	Strategic Planning		
Vision →	Transform, Innovate, Stabilize, Grow		
Strategy →	Operations Strategy		
Objectives →	S.T.A.R.	S.M.A.R.T. Goals	Operations Process
Goals →	Utilize a four-step process to develop and implement a strategic plan	Write S.M.A.R.T. Goals	Define two Objectives that address small business operations
Tactics →	Use the S.T.A.R. process to develop an action plan Define a S.O.D. for your business Implement a strategic planning process	Write goals Review goals Rewrite goals if necessary	Select two objectives aligned with Operations Strategy Write goals, tactics and results to address the objective
Results →	S.T.A.R. Answers	S.M.A.R.T. Goals	Operations Strategy

Strategic Planning for Existing Businesses

With an intense schedule to meet and the time constraints of a business, small business owners learn quickly how to prioritize their needs taking into consideration their strengths and weaknesses. To sustain growth they learn how to validate their strategic direction. They understand the importance of what can be delegated or out-sourced and what should be maintained for strategic advantage. They identify and document important decisions to ensure a strong structural foundation for their business's long-term survival. Small business owners become familiar with the resources available that can add to their own wealth of knowledge and assist in their continued success. Concepts we address in this book include:

- Strategic decision-making skills
- Transformational operations
- Innovative entrepreneurial roles
- Stabilized financial methodologies
- Sustainable growth and marketing your business
- Profitability for survival and beyond

To take your business to the next level, follow the steps in the S.T.A.R. process to build and implement a strategic plan. Ask yourself key questions as you review your strategic plan.

1. **Strategize** – Does your plan connect with the vision that you have for your organization? What is important to you? What is your focus? Have you completed a S.O.D. (Strengths, Opportunities, and Dangers)?

2. **Target (Planning)** – How are you going to implement the strategy? Where are you going to assign your resources? Are your S.M.A.R.T. goals written down?

3. **Act** – What initiatives have you implemented to align your organization with the strategies you defined? How are you implementing your plan? Are you aligning your resources to your strategic plan?

4. **Reflect** – What is the impact on the organization? What needs to be changed? What challenges and obstacles might you face when you implement your plan? What are your outcomes?

Repeat the same steps each time you focus on a new business strategy. As you build your plan include strategies that focus on transforming, innovating, stabilizing, and growing your business. Continue to use the S.T.A.R. process to achieve your vision.

Strategic Planning – Creating Sustainable Success includes the following outcomes designed to ensure sustainable growth.

- **One-Page Strategic Plan (1-PSP)**

  A strategic plan designed for your small business to survive and take it to the next level.

- **One-Page Relationship Chart (1-PRC)**

  A list of key individuals who are essential to the organization.

- **12-Month Cash Flow (12-MCF)**

  A financial plan to enhance profits through increasing income and decreasing expenses.

- **Seven-Touch Marketing Plan (7-TMP)**

  A marketing plan to ensure that your message reaches your target market.

- **One-Page Action Plan (1-PAP)**

  A detailed plan that includes available funding and who is responsible to implement the strategic initiatives defined in the 1-PSP.

Pay attention to what matters most and transform, innovate, stabilize, and grow your business to achieve sustainable success using a S.T.A.R. planning cycle – Strategize, Target, Act, and Reflect.

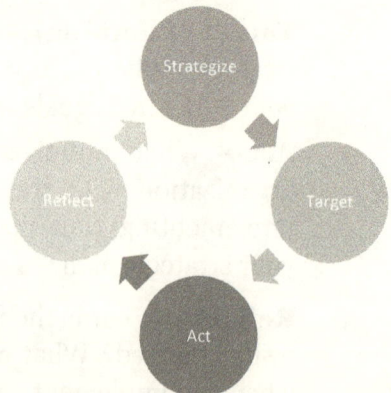

Strategic Planning (1-PSP)

The One-Page Strategic Plan (1-PSP) was developed as a single-page instrument by Joanne Osmond and Claudia Pannell to keep the purpose and direction of the organization in the forefront of an individual's mind. A 1-PSP is generally colorful in appearance to aid in recall and to make it stand out in a stack of papers. Recent conventions encourage lamination to avoid accidental loss or destruction. While laminated pieces may be difficult to throw away, some feel it also makes them a strong candidate for continued use. Although debatable, lamination generally stands the test of time.

The general concept of the 1-PSP is closely tied to an organization's documented goals. While the goal documents are further detailed with tactics, timeframes, measurements, and results, the 1-PSP summarizes the direction of the goals and ties them directly to the organization's strategic direction. Generally speaking, goal documents may be multiple pages almost entirely in pure text, but the 1-PSP is, by design, a single page with colorful geometric designs. The simpler the organization and design, the more likely the content will be remembered which is a primary goal of the 1-PSP.

Components of the 1-PSP can vary according to the situation or area of the business using it; but generally speaking, each contains the following elements:

- Company Name
- Vision
- Strategies
- Objectives
- Goals
- Tactics
- Results

Formatting the elements in a standard design helps share understanding and quick recall.

Using Word, Excel, or PowerPoint, the design generally appears in a chart format.

1-PSP (One-Page Strategic Plan)

Company Name

Vision

People		Operations		Finance		Marketing	
Objective	Objective	Objective	Objective	Objective	Objective	Objective	Objective
Goal	Goal	Goal	Goal	Goal	Goal	Goal	Goal
Tactics	Tactics	Tactics	Tactics	Tactics	Tactics	Tactics	Tactics
Result	Result	Result	Result	Result	Result	Result	Result

Taking a closer look at each of the element areas, it becomes obvious how the goals and 1-PSP document relate to one another.

Company Name – This may appear self-explanatory, but the fact is, many organizations either purposely omit their name, citing confidentiality, or they simply fail to place their name on the document. In either event, a strategic planning document with no company name at the top is unlikely to be taken seriously by those who are expected to use and follow it. Alternately, some organizations make multiple 1-PSP documents listing the company name at the top and the sub-units or functions directly below. When this is the case, it is not uncommon for the corporate plan to be on one side of the document and the functional plan on the other. On the functional side, however, the function name is listed directly below the corporate name in the same area. This is an excellent way to reinforce how the different areas of the business are working strategically toward the same direction.

Vision – By placing the company's vision at the top of the 1-PSP document directly under the company name, it brings clarity and eliminates ambiguity to the strategic plan. This is an important part of the document and must not be omitted. As was the case earlier, it is not uncommon for sub-units or functions to have their own area's vision statement which aligns appropriately to the corporate vision. Where this is the case, it would be acceptable to place the functional vision, without the corporate vision, on the functional side of the document. Record your vision in the top box on page 23.

There are three basic types of businesses (with lots of variations): 1) innovative products and services, 2) low-cost providers, and 3) personalized services. The classic innovative provider is 3M where they continually invest profits in developing new products. The classic low-cost provider is Wal-Mart. While we cannot be all things to all people, we can pick one model and excel at it. Most small businesses do not attempt to compete with 3M and Wal-Mart; however, they excel at customer service. Small businesses know their customers and they can keep their customers' needs in mind at all times. When I walk into my favorite restaurant and the waitress walks up with my favorite drink, I will pay more. That is a vision!

Strategies – The strategies are the outcome of a business strategic planning session and may adjust slightly over time as the business environments change. They indicate areas where the company feels emphasis must be placed to build or sustain competitive advantage. Quite often these areas are identified through exercises like S.O.D. (Strengths, Opportunities, and Dangers). As strategic components of a competitive advantage, the strategies may cross functional boundaries and become key elements that bind a company's strategic plan. In a large organization, it would be unusual for functional areas not to have identical strategies with the parent company.

Most small businesses focus on four strategic areas: People, Operations, Finance, and Marketing.

Objectives – Objectives support the strategies in building and sustaining a competitive advantage. They are much more specific than the strategies and may or may not cross functional boundaries. In some cultures, objectives and goals are terms which are used interchangeably. In the 1-PSP, objectives serve the purpose of being the overarching category for multiple goals and tactics.

Goals – Goals for any substantial strategic plan will follow the S.M.A.R.T. convention. Whether the 1-PSP is for the corporate or the functional area of the business, the goals are listed below the corresponding objective. When specific goals are shared across functional lines, these goals will be documented under each area and marked with an asterisk (*). It is also very important that the language of the goal is the same across the functional lines. If not, ambiguity can arise and the best result may be a half-completed goal. For this reason, shared goals are usually written jointly with management approval before they are finally established.

Tactics – Tactics take up the majority of space on the document. It is not uncommon for them to take up to one-half of the page. Tactics are very specific and end with the expected completion dates or time periods. Some organizations find it helpful to put tactics in chronological order to make it easier to identify at a glance what should be occurring at any given time. However, this may not be an exercise worth the effort, considering that there are not an excessive number of tactics which can be included on one-half of a page. Furthermore, tactics and due dates are tracked and measured on the One-Page Action Plan (1-PAP). The 1-PAP (explained in the last section of this book) is a clearer way to display the status of tactics. It is a typical dashboard document or high-level summary with red, yellow, and green indicators of progress.

Results – Results are the indicators that the objectives have been met. It is how you know that you are done. It is important for the organization to know when they can celebrate and when they need to work harder to achieve the end results. Results can be tracked on the 1-PAP or scorecard with color-coded indicators to monitor progress. Results must be tangible and clear so there is no uncertainty when success is achieved.

The 1-PSP (One-Page Strategic Plan) is an extremely important document for any business. It is a basic building block in developing and sustaining the success of the business. The attractiveness of design and ease-of-use functionality makes it a powerful tool for any business owner. It can be used to keep everyone in the business literally on the same page. The 1-PSP can demonstrate clear direction when discussing business affairs with bankers, attorneys, accountants, and other business associates.

While we provide a model for the 1-PSP, there are other formats that may be more useful depending on the situation. For a small group or team, sticky notes placed strategically on areas of the wall can be an effective tool when developing the 1-PSP.

A whiteboard with multi-color dry erase markers can also be used as the 1-PSP is evolving. Even a large piece of butcher paper can be utilized in the formative stage. Regardless of the method to develop the 1-PSP, the final product should be reduced to a size that all employees can have as a personal copy to review frequently. The objective is not to develop a wall chart to display in a common area but to involve all stakeholders and ensure buy-in on the objectives. Everyone needs a constant reminder of what needs to be completed to reach the targets. The final document should be whatever will motivate the business owner and the employees.

1-PSP (One-Page Strategic Plan)

Fine Dining Tonight

Delivering a Superior Dining Experience

	People		Operations		Finance		Marketing	
	OSHA Compliance	Employee Retention	Technology	Food Quality	Cash Flow	Purchasing	Website	Customer Loyalty
	100% of staff are trained in Kitchen Safety by 3/31	Employee Satisfaction Survey Written by 4/15	Upgrade main entrance to reflect image and security concerns by 8/1	Review customer satisfaction surveys for suggestions by 3/1	Manage cash flow to build reserve by end of 1st quarter	Develop schedule for purchasing staples by 9/1	Complete redesign of Web site by 10/1	Prepare customer discount cards to distribute in December by 11/1
	Kitchen safety training program by 1/15	Select questions for survey by 2/1	Research security cameras by 1/15	Organize surveys by 9/1	Determine goal by 2/1	Select product by 6/1	Review current site by 5/1	Design cards by 9/1
	Kitchen safety program by 2/1	Determine methodology for survey by 4/1	Write RFP by 1/20	Review food quality comments by 10/1	Open account by 2/15	Determine storage and useful life by 8/1	Determine improvements by 5/15	Submit art work to printer by 10/1
	Kitchen safety program by 2/15	Distribute survey by 6/1	Award contract by 2/10	Make suggestions by 11/1	Deposit $ monthly	Develop schedule by 9/1	Select Web designer by 6/1	Include card in December mailing by 12/1
	Pass Health Department Inspection	95% Retention	0% Citations	95% on Survey	$ in Reserve	95% On Time	100% Complete	50% Cards Used

S.M.A.R.T. Goals

Generally speaking, when individuals reference the term "smart" while simultaneously addressing goals, they are referring to the acronym S.M.A.R.T. Over time, this acronym has had a variety of definitions, but the most accepted include the five common characteristics of a goal. Some would go so far as to say a well-defined goal can only be a S.M.A.R.T. goal.

The origin of S.M.A.R.T. goals is not known, however, many point to Peter Drucker's 1954 classic titled *The Practice of Management*.

In his book, there is a reference to similar characteristics where Drucker discusses object-based management. Drucker is not the only person addressing goals in reference to objectives. Many individuals familiar with project management are acutely aware of the need to define objectives in a fashion easily translated to a diverse team working on a particular project. They also have found success in the use of S.M.A.R.T. goals.

The words used to create the acronym have also been widely debated and varied; but again, generally speaking, they have been narrowed down to the following:

S   –   Specific
M   –   Measurable
A   –   Attainable
R   –   Relevant
T   –   Time-bound

When defining a goal, the primary objective should be to answer the following questions: 1) What are we trying to accomplish? 2) How will we know whether or not we are successful? and 3) What is the result if we are not successful? This is where the S.M.A.R.T. definitions are the most powerful. Done correctly, they are the guidelines for making sure the goals are complete when written.

To get a better understanding, the terms or words of the S.M.A.R.T. acronym must be defined in more detail.

'S'pecific is the part of the goal that describes the What, the Why, and the How of the goal. The focus is on the effort and the expectation of the goal. It has often been said that when a goal is specific, it is written in a manner in which your grandmother would be able to understand it, regardless of the type of business involved. An example of a non-specific goal might be: 'Modernize the office.'

Ask yourself these three questions – What, Why, and How? If the goal as written can answer those questions, you are on your way to a specific goal. In this example, assumptions could be made as to the answers, but that defeats the purpose. Said another way, there should be no ambiguity when the goal is written.

A better goal might be:

> 'Upgrade the reception area at the main office to reflect a positive image and a commitment to security awareness by the end of first quarter, 2011.'

Again, by asking the three questions, we understand the 'What' to be an upgrade of the reception area at the main office. This is very specific and there is no ambiguity. The 'Why' is clearly to reflect a positive image and commitment to security awareness. This describes a specific focus for the efforts of this goal. Finally, the 'How' identifies that this goal is to be completed by a very specific time and date. Can it be finished earlier than the end of the first quarter? Of course it can. However, there is no confusion in that it MUST be completed by a specific date, March 31, 2011.

'M'easurable describes the steps or the approach that will be taken to accomplish the goal. These are the individual parts that make up the 'What' of the goal and are monitored at the lowest level in the plan to demonstrate whether or not progress is being made towards a successful completion of the goal. Ultimately, this is the source of success or failure and can be visualized as links in the chain of the process. Remember the old adage "a goal is only as strong as its weakest link."

Using our same example, a non-measurable goal or tactic might be: 'Modernize the office.'

To understand measurable, ask the question, "What will this goal look like when it has been completed successfully?" Does the phrase 'Modernize the office' look the same to everyone when completed? Hardly! One person might see a new throw rug at the front door. Another may see a completely remodeled area with twice the space! Ambiguity with no measurable criteria does not foster success.

The better goal example was 'Upgrade the reception area at the main office to reflect a positive image and a commitment to security awareness by the end of first quarter, 2011.'

Good tactics for this goal might be:

- Research security cameras for the reception area at the main office by 1/15/11.
- Write RFP for security cameras by 1/20/11.
- Award contract for security camera installation by 2/10/11.
- Security cameras installed and working successfully by 3/1/11.
- Staff trained on the use, response, and support of security cameras by 3/15/11.

Referring back to the goal, notice that the tactics above only represent a portion of the goal. Tactics should be written to address the 'positive image' portion of the upgrade. These could include such things as researching architects or interior designers, etc.

'A'ttainable is the part of the goal which motivates success. This is not to be confused with or used interchangeably with the term 'easy.' Most of the time, attainable is slightly out of immediate grasp but not so far out as to be impossible to achieve within given constraints. If a goal is written which is known to be 'easy,' it is more likely to be a routine task or a delegable activity. An 'attainable' goal requires planning and should be expected to be achieved with the support of all functions required to make it successful.

Generally, this means the goal is within the business's strategic direction, is fully funded, and has committed resources (personnel, equipment, executive support, etc.). Additionally, this is the area where project management seeks to obtain 'buy-in' from project stakeholders.

Using our example, the non-attainable goal might be: 'Modernize the office.'

Again, ask the question, "What will the success of this goal look like?" Some may say, replace the light bulbs and you are done! Others may visualize selling the current plant and building in a foreign country! The ambiguity underscores that the goal is not attainable. If there is any doubt, consider whether or not your grandmother would be able to attain the goal as written.

The better goal example was 'Upgrade the reception area at the main office to reflect a positive image and a commitment to security awareness by the end of first quarter, 2011.' To be attainable, the goal should be assigned across the multiple functions of the organization which will be, in part, responsible for its success. In this case, Executive Management, Finance, HR, Facilities, and Security, at a minimum, should participate in this as a shared goal. Additionally, IT, Purchasing, and Sales may have a shared interest.

'R'elevant goals drive a business's mission and its vision. It has often been said that if a goal is not contributing directly to a business's bottom line, it is not worth pursuing. While a company's bottom line is indeed important, sometimes it is not the only thing worthy of a goal. For example, it could be said that compliance goals do not contribute to a firm's bottom line. However, without compliance goals, a firm could be out of business with a 'shut-down' order from the governing agency over their activities.

In our example, the non-relevant goal is: 'Modernize the office.'

The question here is how does this goal improve our business, grow our sales, or make us a better company? More precisely, how does this goal relate to our mission? The answer is again unclear. Some may think a modern image will boost sales. Some may think a modernized office will improve employee morale. The ambiguity makes it very confusing.

The better goal example was 'Upgrade the reception area at the main office to reflect a positive image and a commitment to security awareness by the end of first quarter, 2011.'

The relevance may still be unclear. In order to eliminate all confusion, the goal must be tied to the company's strategic focus. This is identified on the One-Page Strategic Plan (1-PSP).

'T'ime-bound is exactly as it sounds. This portion of the goal is very explicit in when the goal is expected to be completed. Although seldom spelled out, it also implies that the goal will be completed successfully by the time stated. This is often the easiest part in writing a S.M.A.R.T. goal and the most overlooked. It is also why it is a good idea to have others read over the goals to validate that they are clear, free of ambiguity, and follow the S.M.A.R.T. convention.

In our example, the non-time-bound goal is: 'Modernize the office.'

At first glance, it may appear that this is obviously not time-bound. However, remember that when writing goals, it is easy to leave out what may be assumed by others. For example, if it has been clearly announced from top management that in the near future, employees will be seeing evidence of new construction around the office, the above goal may seem adequate. The truth is that one can never assume anything. Remember, would your grandmother know when the goal was going to be complete by reading the above statement? Probably not!

The better goal example was 'Upgrade the reception area at the main office to reflect a positive image and a commitment to security awareness by the end of first quarter, 2011.' Assuming the writing of this goal is some time in the fourth quarter, 2010, and that work on the goal is to start January 1, 2011, then on the surface this goal appears time-bound.

The test of being time-bound is looking into the tactics discussed earlier. This becomes a part of good project planning where the individual steps are planned out in great detail and the timeline is worked backwards to assure successful completion is feasible. If it is not found feasible, then the goal should be rewritten to fit the appropriate timeframe.

S.M.A.R.T. goals are the basic building blocks to keep a business focused on the activities necessary for sustainable success.

They remove barriers of confusion and indecisiveness. Once understood and practiced, they become a fundamental part of everyday business. Like any good habit, success breeds continued use and focus.

Objectives are not S.M.A.R.T.

Objectives are general and similar to headers in a book. They are also Achievable and Relevant but they are neither Measureable nor Time-bound. A simple way to identify Objectives is to consider them GAR-(MT) or General, Achievable, Relevant minus Measureable and Time-bound.

Examples of GAR-(MT) Objectives are:

- Office Modernization
- Entrance Security
- OSHA Compliance
- Employee Retention

Notice that the examples are broad areas that require S.M.A.R.T. goals to define them and provide clarity to what is expected. They are, however, more specific than Strategies.

Future Business Goals

A strategic plan is a collection of business goals that guide the business as it grows and expands. Priorities are set and realistic deliverables defined. Goals should be S.M.A.R.T. – Specific, Measurable, Achievable, Relevant, and Time-bound.

A five-year game plan similar to the 1-PSP is a strategic plan that is formatted on one page for easy reference. The first step is to clarify the vision and the mission for the organization. The vision is where you want to be in five years. It is not who you are but where you want to be. The mission is how you are going to accomplish the five-year vision. It is the key to successfully reaching the destination established in the vision. Strategies are the practical directives that support the mission.

The plan includes a maximum of five strategies. To accomplish the strategies, no more than six objectives (strategic objectives) are defined. The goals that define the objectives are specific, with measurable results produced while implementing strategies. The next step includes identifying specific tasks to implement the goals. The tasks are assigned to an individual who is responsible to complete the task by a specified date. The 1-PSP and five-year strategic plan are similar in form but with a different focus. One looks at the here and now, the other to the future and what you want to accomplish in five years.

What do you want to accomplish in five years?

What are some of your future goals? Include them on a five-year game plan.

1-PSP (One-Page Strategic Plan)

	Marketing		

	Finance		

	Operations		

	People		

Process Overview

This process is designed to provide you with the tools to complete a 1-PSP (One-Page Strategic Plan) and a 1-PAP (One-Page Action Plan). The process starts with Strategize, the high-level planning step of S.T.A.R., to identify what needs to be done. Then Target to work out the details and document the steps to implement the plan. A strategic plan that sits on the shelf and looks pretty is of no value. An action plan written on a napkin that is acted on and implemented can be worth its weight in gold, if the actions are linked to a well-thought-out strategy.

We guide you through a series of steps to delve into each segment of the 1-PSP. It is not something that can be written in an hour. It takes time to focus on what needs to be done and in what order.

Step 1: Organization S.O.D. – At several points in the process you will be asked to complete a S.O.D. (Strengths, Opportunities, Dangers) starting with one for the organization. Begin by identifying your organization's strengths (what it does well, assets it has, special talents, and unique selling propositions), opportunities (new options for growth, new venture capital, potential customers, and new products) and dangers (competitors, legal climate, economy, family situation, etc.)

Step 2: Strategic Planning – A well-thought-out S.O.D. will help you identify areas that can be included in a strategic plan. Begin collecting ideas for your strategic plan and recording them in the space provided on page 31. Come back to the page and continue to record potential goals. Do not spend time at this point making detailed plans or making definitive decisions about what to include on the strategic plan. It is a placeholder for ideas that come during discussions or when reading the material provided.

Step 3: 1-PSP – At this point you should have already started to work on your 1-PSP. The organization's name and vision should be entered in the space indicated at the top of the form. Small businesses are different in many ways but very similar in others.

The four strategies that cover all organizations are: People, Operations, Finance, and Marketing. Based on your business and preferences, operations will be very diverse while the other three will have more similarities in objectives and even goals.

Step 4: Strategies – For each strategy, the same process is used to clarify the strategy (People, Operations, Finance, and Marketing) and build the 1-PSP. Using the tools provided assists in identifying the objectives, goals, tactics, and results for each strategy.

S.O.D. – Each strategic session will begin with a S.O.D. for that specific strategy. From the S.O.D. you can select two objectives as the highest priority. When one objective under a strategy is completed, another can be selected for the same strategy. Strategic Planning is a continuous cycle. As one goal is accomplished another takes its place.

Objectives – Objectives are like chapter headings, only one or two words. They are not measured or time-bound. They are general and serve as a focus for the goal that falls beneath the objective.

Goals – Goals are specific, measurable, and include a timeframe. They follow the objectives and lead to tactics and results.

For each strategy use the appropriate tool then identify the objectives, goals, tactics, and results that are associated with the strategy. As you drill down and focus on specific strategies (People, Operations, Finance, and Marketing) additional tools are available to simplify the process of identifying objectives, goals, tactics, and results.

1-PRC – The One-Page Relationship Chart on page 30 looks at specific individuals, including their roles in the organization, their similarities and differences, their value to your organization, and specific ways you can work to improve the relationship. It is important to focus on developing a highly-qualified team of professionals. A One-Page Relationship Chart will assist in identifying ways to build stronger connections between the members of your team, your employees, your customers, your vendors, and other stakeholders.

12-MCF – The Twelve-Month Cash Flow Statement is vital to small business owners. While strategic planning includes other financial statements and a brief discussion on ratios, it is the 12-Month Cash Flow that is the most important.

7-TMP – A Seven-Touch Marketing Plan helps to build multiple channels to reach your target market. The magic number of touches before a customer will be comfortable buying your product or service is seven. Are you reaching your target market to tell your story?

After the **1-PSP** is complete, it is used to create an action plan to ensure that the goals are implemented and success achieved.

1-PAP – The One-Page Action Plan looks at the tactics and adds key information such as responsibility and cost. Using the **1-PAP** you can identify the critical path and define which tactics must be completed in what order to achieve the desired results. It also serves as a scorecard to monitor the tasks 'completed,' 'in process,' or 'not started.'

The **1-PAP** includes one page for each objective. If you are working as a team, you can give team members just the **1-PAP** that they need to complete their initiative. When updated regularly, it provides an effective means of communicating the progress of the strategic plan.

At any point in the process, please contact us with your questions and concerns: Instructor@SmallBusinessSpokenHere.com. If you are working with an advisor, please continue to ask them for advice on setting goals and creating a strategic plan.

Information is available at www.SmallBusinessSpokenHere.com. All of the documents and materials for strategic planning in PDF format can be downloaded from the site.

1-PSP Activity

The small business strategic planning process begins by looking at your business from the top down. What are those big tasks that you need to complete as an organization?

Business / Organization S.O.D. (Strengths, Opportunities, Dangers)

Your strengths may be in one area (excellent product and service) and your opportunities may be in marketing, but with practice you can balance your 1-PSP and identify objectives for all of the strategic areas. We provide you with tools to identify objectives and goals to achieve successful results. List below your company strengths and opportunities plus any dangers or threats to your organization.

Strengths	
Opportunities	
Dangers	

Strategic Exercise

Brainstorm ideas for your organization based on the S.O.D. that you completed and on an understanding of your organization's purpose.

Define the purpose, mission, and vision of your organization

```
┌─────────────────────────────────────────────┐
│                                             │
│                                             │
│                                             │
│                                             │
└─────────────────────────────────────────────┘
```

Potential Goals that concern the operations of your business

```
┌─────────────────────────────────────────────┐
│                                             │
│                                             │
│                                             │
│                                             │
└─────────────────────────────────────────────┘
```

Potential Goals that involve people and relationships

```
┌─────────────────────────────────────────────┐
│                                             │
│                                             │
│                                             │
│                                             │
└─────────────────────────────────────────────┘
```

Potential Finance Goals

```
┌─────────────────────────────────────────────┐
│                                             │
│                                             │
│                                             │
│                                             │
└─────────────────────────────────────────────┘
```

Potential Marketing Goals

```
┌─────────────────────────────────────────────┐
│                                             │
│                                             │
│                                             │
│                                             │
└─────────────────────────────────────────────┘
```

If you have not already done so, write your organization's name and vision on a 1-PSP Worksheet.

Examples of Strategic Planning Forms

One-Page Strategic Plan (1-PSP)

A strategic plan designed for a small business to take their business to the next level.

1-PSP (One-Page Strategic Plan)   Date: 5/1/2010

Forbidden Sweets

Hand crafted, hand dipped and decorated with our unique designs

People		Operations		Finance		Marketing	
Staff Training	Vendor Recognition	Niche Product	Warm Weather Shipping	Cash Flow	Inventory	Target Market	Wholesale
Training additional staff by 12/1	Identify methods of recognizing vendors by 3/1	Identify specific products by 4/15	Determine summer shipping method by 4/1	Monitor Cash Flow weekly by 9/1	Install inventory tracking system by 11/1	Identify retailers by 4/1	Identify potential wholesalers by 9/1
Define processes and procedures by 10/1 / Write training instructions by 11/1 / Set training dates by 11/1 / Prepare Materials for training by 11/15	List vendors by 2/1 / Select recognition by 2/15 / Write thank you by 1/20 / Make or purchase recognitions by 2/20 / Deliver to vendors in 3/1	Identify best selling products by 1/1 / Determine cost and additional inventory need to make product by 1/15 / Design product(s) by 2/15 / Order materials 3/1	Contact shippers 1/15 / Purchase materials by 2/1 / Compare cost by 2/15 / Test methods by 4/1	Update QuickBooks immediately upon receipt of invoices and submission of bills by 8/1 / Run QuickBooks reports weekly by 8/15 / Review weekly Cash Flow by 9/1	Identify inventory software by 5/1 / Test and review specs for software by 7/1 / Select software by 8/1 / Transition to new product by 9/1 / Run tests by 10/1	Identify additional retailers to target by 1/1 / Define 7-Touch Plan to reach retailers by 2/1 / Develop materials and resources needed to complete 7-TMP by 3/15 / Implement Plan by 4/1	Identify potential wholesalers by 6/1 / Define 7-Touch Plan to reach retailers by 7/1 / Develop materials and resources needed to complete 7-TMP by 8/15 / Implement Plan by 9/1
Training session by 12/1	Recognition delivered in March	Select top sellers by 4/15	Summer Shipping Process by 4/1	Weekly Cash Flow Reports by 9/1	New Inventory System by 11/1	7-TMP for Retailers by 2/1	7-TMP for Wholesalers by 9/1

The 1-PSP summarizes the organization's goals and ties them directly to the strategies. A 1-PSP is a single page with components that can vary according to the situation or area of the business using it; but generally speaking, each contains the following elements: Company Name, Vision, Strategies, Objectives, Goals, Tactics, and Results.

The 1-PSP is a one-page reminder of what the organization has defined as important. It sets priorities and direction to accomplish the most important goals and drives the organization to success.

One-Page Relationship Chart (1-PRC) – A list of key individuals who are essential to the organization.

1-PRC (One-Page Relationship Chart)

Name	Role	Differences	Similarities	Value	Objective
John Doe	Chocolate Supplier	Quiet, Cautious		Excellent customer service	Be patient and provide information in writing
Mary Smith	Packaging Supplier	Creative, Outgoing	Open, honest	Great new ideas	Listen to ideas, implement the best
Patty Pleasant	UPS Driver		Prompt	Always on time	Thank Driver
Tiny Tim	Wholesaler		Practical, down-to-earth, no nonsense	Gets the job done	Refer Wholesaler to other manufacturers
Jane Brawn	Partner	Analytical	Data Driven	Knows exactly what needs to be done	Provide feedback on data

12-Month Cash Flow (12-MCF) – A financial plan to enhance profits through increasing income and decreasing expenses.

12 - Month Cash Flow

	1/1/2010 Month 1	2/1/2010 Month 2	3/1/2010 Month 3	4/1/2010 Month 4	5/1/2010 Month 5	6/1/2010 Month 6	7/1/2010 Month 7	8/1/2010 Month 8	9/1/2010 Month 9	10/1/2010 Month 10	11/1/2010 Month 11	12/1/2010 Month 12	Year 1 TOTAL
Beg. Cash	16,521	16,668	23,298	30,980	42,985	68,970	85,447	97,435	98,795	99,111	102,562	108,586	16,521
Receipts	22,933	32,657	29,231	36,432	56,096	42,893	32,398	25,231	18,584	24,482	28,890	38,438	383,265
Loan	0	0	0	0	0	0	0	0	0	0	0	0	0
Equity	0	0	0	0	0	0	0	0	0	0	0	0	0
TOTAL CASH	39,454	49,325	52,529	67,392	99,081	111,863	117,845	117,666	117,379	123,593	131,452	147,024	399,786
COGS1	8,589	10,089	7,436	9,546	11,489	9,845	7,659	5,892	5,489	7,859	8,209	10,973	100,477
Officer's Salary	5,000	5,000	5,000	5,000	5,000	5,000	5,000	5,000	5,000	5,000	5,000	5,000	60,000
Sales Payroll Expense	2,038	3,285	2,598	2,895	4,675	3,987	1,765	2,038	2,038	2,038	2,598	2,994	32,949
Payroll Taxes	883	1100	870	970	1586	1336	591	683	683	683	870	1003	11,038
Rent	650	650	650	650	650	650	650	650	650	650	650	650	7,800
Utilities	300	418	357	389	490	400	365	280	257	317	353	388	4,313
Telephone	57	78	59	63	98	75	60	57	57	57	59	67	787
Maintenance	195	74	83	92	198	57	39	41	192	87	69	94	1,221
Insurance	273	273	273	273	273	273	273	273	273	273	273	273	3,276
Advertising	559	521	686	798	852	689	532	321	300	495	642	548	6,943
Office Expense	87	200	57	32	90	187	73	54	39	194	45	96	1,158
Supplies	69	0	0	53	0	0	0	0	62	0	0	93	277
Professional Fees	314	450	0	0	280	0	0	295	0	0	310	0	1,649
Bank Charges	108	98	115	89	97	132	129	125	118	89	102	132	1,331
Travel & Entertain	375	93	82	57	278	86	73	54	109	189	176	210	1,782
Furniture & Fixture	132	0	0	0	0	0	0	0	0	0	0	0	132
Equipment	1859	0	0	0	0	0	0	0	0	0	0	0	1,859
Misc or 10% contingency	2,000	2,200	1,800	2,000	2,600	2,200	1,700	1,600	1,500	1,800	2,000	2,200	23,600
TOTAL EXPENSE	21,286	24,527	20,068	22,907	28,611	24,917	18,909	17,372	16,768	18,531	21,306	24,330	260,692
NET CASH OUTLAY	18,168	24,798	32,480	44,485	70,470	86,947	98,935	100,295	100,611	104,062	110,086	122,694	139,194
Loan	1,500	1,500	1,500	1,500	1,500	1,500	1,500	1,500	1,500	1,500	1,500	1,500	18,000
END CASH	16,668	23,298	30,980	42,985	68,970	85,447	97,435	98,795	99,111	102,562	108,586	121,194	121,194

Seven-Touch Marketing Plan (7-TMP) – A marketing plan to ensure that your message reaches the target market.

Target Market	Retail Stores (Card Shops)

	Method	Description	Frequency	Cost
1	Letter	Write a letter of introduction to area card shop owners, introducing company and products by 8/1	1	$25.00
2	Phone Call	Follow-up phone call to area card shops by 9/1	Multiple – to talk to decision maker	$0.00
3	Personal Contact	Drop off sample product (or mail sample) to Card Shops by 10/1	1 (may require multiple visits)	$50.00
4	Brochure	Deliver or send catalog of products by 10/1	1 (may require additional materials)	$100.00
5	Monthly e-newsletter	Use Constant Contact to send link to Web site by 10/15	Monthly	$10.00
6	Reference	Send personal e-mail with reference and comments from customers who they can contact by 11/15	1	$0.00
7	Display Unit	Deliver or send display unit with sample product by 12/1	1	$10.00
Total Cost				$195.00

One-Page Action Plan (1-PAP)

A detailed plan that includes available funding and who is responsible to implement the strategic initiatives defined in the 1-PSP.

1-PAP (One-Page Action Plan)

Strategy   *Operations*

Objective   *Successfully ship product in bulk in summer months*   Completion Date: *March 1*

Goal	Tactic	Completion Date	Responsibility	Cost	Result	Achieved (Yes / No)	
By April 1st determine shipping methodology for product shipped in the summer so that it arrives at its destination in excellent condition without any defects or discoloration 100% of the time.	1. Contact carriers – FEDEX, UPS, USPS – Request shipping instructions / Recommendations.	January 1	Roxanne	$0	Shipping recommendations	Yes	
	2. Purchase packaging materials as recommended by carrier.	February 1	Roxanne	$50	Packaging options		
	3. Research additional packaging materials on Internet and through other sources such as ULine.	January 15	Roxanne	$0	Additional shipping recommendations		
	4. Purchase any other materials available that are recommended that will prevent product from overheating.	February 1	Roxanne	$50	Additional packaging options		
	5. Compare cost of options.	February 15	Roxanne	$0	Cost Matrix		

The 1-PAP shows in a glance what is completed, what is in process, and what tasks you have not started.

The set of easy-to-use tools provides a framework to assist in building a successful strategic plan for your small business.

SMALL BUSINESS STRATEGIC PLANNING

Operations Strategic Planning

Every business has a unique operation. While they are one of a kind, it is easy for a business owner to see what needs to be done to improve the way the organization runs.

1. Start with an Operations S.O.D. Look at your product and services. Decide what needs to be done differently. What projects are important to your success? What are your product strengths? What opportunities do you have to improve or expand your product offering? What new approaches will make a difference? What are the dangers if you do not try innovative new solutions? Your Operations S.O.D. will begin to trigger ideas that will be used in your **1-PSP**.

2. Select two objectives and define S.M.A.R.T. goals that can help you achieve your objectives.

3. List tactics or steps to take in achieving the broader goal.

4. The final step is to define what success looks like and list it as the result.

Operations S.O.D. (Strengths, Opportunities, Dangers)

Strengths	
Opportunities	
Dangers	

Ideas for Operations Objectives and Goals

Business	Objective	Goal
Web Design	Technology	Improve the server capacity to accommodate business expansion by December 31st.
Restaurant	Menu	Revise menu to provide more gluten-free choices by August 1st.
Cleaning Service	Products	Evaluate the new 'Green' line of cleaning solutions for effectiveness by May 1st.
Consulting	Development	Attend users' conference to learn new concepts by September 1st.
Bicycle Shop	Expansion	Open second location near lake for summer rentals by April 15th.
Landscaping	Equipment	Identify, analyze, and purchase equipment to provide backups when current equipment is in shop for repairs by September 30th.
Oil Lube Franchise	Additions	Open two new bays for express lubes by January 1st.
Bowling Alley	Repairs	Refinish and repair first 20 lanes by May 1st.
Children's Party Center	Products	Add new line of inflatable obstacle courses for the pre-school and elementary age group.
Custom Jewelry	Vendors	Locate a minimum of 3 new vendors with design locations in South America, Israel, and Africa by November 1st.
Security Surveillance	Technology	Upgrade cameras and include new surveillance certification software by July 1st.
Machine Tooling	Raw Materials	Identify several new sources for potential expansion by February 15th.
Painting Contractor	Supplies	Restock supply of sample products to use in custom interior painting jobs for customers to select from by August 1st.
Trucking	Maintenance	Create new maintenance schedule for OTR tractors for compliance with new federal laws by January 1st.
Custom-made Dolls	Product Line	Sketch-out potential new product line of Children's T-shirts and caps by April 30th.
Fruit Juice Retailer	Farmer's Market	Add 4 new Farmer's Markets to current list and have contracts signed, booths paid, and equipment scheduled by March 1st.

Operations Strategy

Objectives

Goals

Tactics

Results

Transform ~ **Innovate** ~ Stabilize ~ Grow

People Strategy

Using the 1-PSP format, the outcomes for chapter two are listed below.

Strategic Planning

Innovation

People Strategy

S.T.A.R.	Leadership	Relationships	Networking
Utilize a four step process to develop and implement a 1-PRC	Increase the organization's innovation capacity	Identify key relationships	Understand, Ask, Listen, and Share Networking
Use S.T.A.R. process (Strategize, Target, Act, and Reflect) to create 1-PRC	Identify steps to increase innovation in organization Provide funding Sustain and reward innovation	List key relationships Recognize preferences Identify actions to strengthen relationship Complete 1-PRC	List questions to ask when networking Compile list of resources you might share if they are needed Identify needs at networking events
1-PRC	Innovative Goals	Effective Relationships	1-PSP People Strategy

People Strategy

Building relationships with your team of professionals is only a start at harnessing the power of good relationships. The ability to first understand yourself, and then understand others so you can connect, is the cornerstone of a successful relationship.

A people or relationship S.T.A.R. begins with focusing on the strategic relationships and identifies your role as the leader of your organization. An awareness that differences exist and a willingness to respect others because of their differences enhances the relationship and builds trust.

1. **Strategize** – Who are the members of your team? What are your goals for improving the relationship you have with the key players on your team?

2. **Target** – Have you identified each player's role, how to interact with them, and what you want to achieve by improving relationships? Are your goals S.M.A.R.T.?

3. **Act** – What specific steps are necessary to achieve the goals set above? How are you going to implement your people strategy?

4. **Reflect** – What worked and what did not work? Did you improve the relationship between the most-challenging individuals on the team? What needs to be done differently?

Focusing on others and making sure their needs are met will improve your chances of success. Build strategies around the challenging relationship and whatever needs to be done to improve that relationship. Build a team of professionals that will support you and enhance your entire organization. Incorporate key professionals including a banker, attorney, accountant, insurance agent, and an advisor.

Other key relationships are partners, employees, customers, vendors, peers, and family members. Each plays an important role in the organization's success.

The One-Page Relationship Chart is a tool to assist you in identifying and tracking progress in developing good relationships with key team members.

Name	Role	Differ- ences	Similarities	Value	Actions
John Doe	Chocolate Supplier	Quiet, Cautious		Excellent customer service	Be patient and provide information in writing
Mary Smith	Packaging Supplier	Creative, Outgoing	Open, honest	Great new ideas	Listen to ideas, implement the best
Patty Pleasant	UPS Driver		Prompt	Always on time	Thank Driver
Tiny Tim	Wholesaler		Practical, down-to-earth	Gets the job done	Refer Wholesaler to other manufacturers
Jane Brawn	Partner	Analytical	Data Driven	Knows exactly what needs to be done	Provide feedback on data

The chart includes individuals who are important to your business (attorney, CPA, administrative assistant, forklift driver, etc.) and the role they play in your business or life. Then indentify similarities and differences such as communication preferences, tendency to procrastinate, or ways you approach a project. Include the individual's value to the organization and what actions you plan to take to improve your relationship with the individual. The chart is a tool in defining your People Strategy. It will help you look at the process in innovative ways.

Innovation is essential to opening your mind to new ideas and new ways of working with people.

Innovation in Leading the Way

Innovation is perhaps one of the most critical skills required of the small business owner as the leader of their company. Many times when we think of the term 'innovation' the image of a great inventor or politician or renowned giant of business comes to mind. Sometimes it conjures up the notion of 'thinking outside the box.' The fact is that the term innovation is really a process and like any process, it must be managed well to be successful. There are three primary components that a small business owner must provide if they are to implement innovation within their company.

These components are also the make-up of entrepreneurial leaders. They are: 1) leadership; 2) access to funding; and 3) accountability.

Leadership

A brief review of history teaches us that innovation and transformation occur during times of economic turmoil. Entrepreneurial leaders are the first to spot this phenomenon and seize the opportunities, complete with all the risks that go along with taking that action. They realize that in order to move their business forward, they can no longer carry the weight of the business alone. They look out among those they know and begin to delegate authority, empower their work forces and hire individuals to manage the coming change.

Notice that the entrepreneurial leader needs individuals that can organize and manage the work. As entrepreneurs, they already recognize and understand that they do not need people like themselves who are catalysts in making change happen. They require administrators, supervisors, and other types of management with leadership skills; but do not underestimate the primary need to delegate and empower individuals.

It is one thing to delegate or empower and another to communicate clearly the responsibilities of these individuals. In other words, lip service is unacceptable. Management must know what is expected, when, and by what measures they will be held accountable.

The management team may be less holistic in understanding the big picture and more tactical in their organizing of activities. The entrepreneurial leader must continue to lead innovation from the perspective of the entire organization. If the leader cannot do this, they must accept the fact that it may be time to step aside for the good of the whole.

Business leaders understand that listening to the ideas of their employees, vendors, partners, and customers is one of the best avenues for identifying value-added propositions for their organizations. As our world grows smaller through globalization, this becomes a truth of strategic planning as well as business growth. For innovation to translate into business prosperity, entrepreneurs require leadership skills honed in observation, active listening, focus, and timely responses.

Access to Funding

Innovation is not funded by the hope and aspiration of dreams. It requires a dedicated financial commitment. This does not mean that the entrepreneurial leader must break the bank. What it means is that those who have been given delegation authority, empowerment, and management responsibility clearly understand that an environment has been established which will financially foster innovation.

So the goal is to create an environment where innovation can be nurtured and grown through studying, learning, teaching, failing, and succeeding. The management team and employees must be encouraged to constantly challenge the status quo. They should be asking questions to verify the business is doing the right thing at the right time for the right reasons. When the business environment changes so quickly around us that we forget to stop and take notice, we are doomed to be overtaken by progress. This means we must create a place where we periodically stop and take a close look at what is ahead of us in the industry. Then we have to imagine our business as an active member of that future picture. We have to ask ourselves, what changes must be made now to be better prepared for our business presence in that future picture? Most importantly, what kind of solutions do we see for those changes that must be made?

Once we adapt to this process of continuous innovative thinking, entrepreneurs must train their employees to welcome this environment. We do that through opportunity, reward, recognition, and implementing their successes. When employees are allowed to operate in this fashion, the groundwork for innovation is laid. One way to visually express this concept is shown here and results in what some individuals have coined as 'innovation capacity.'

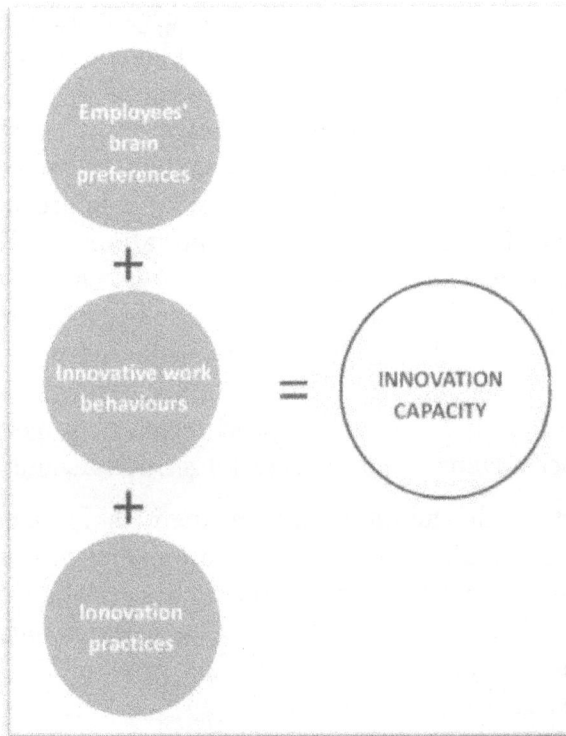

(Image courtesy: www.techmankanata.com)

What is the payoff of creating an environment modeled like the above? Probably the most significant benefit is a higher probability of creating a competitive advantage. Any time a business is able to stay focused on the future and can deliver solutions for the issues that will arise; it will leave the competition behind.

So, if the benefit of innovation can be a competitive advantage with sustainable growth, what is the cost? Going back to what was said earlier; we can now see that the cost is not necessarily in hard dollars for capital expense, but rather an investment in the people of the organization. The costs will be focused on addressing the needs of the employees, preparing them for innovation and change, and tracking the progress as the organization moves forward. Access to funding means implementing an innovation-friendly environment and providing a financial budget in which it can thrive.

Accountability

As the entrepreneurial leader prepares the organization for innovation and change, the third component is not lost on their instinct for success. Success is a measure and to ensure success, measurements must be put in place to gauge the forward progression of the changes the organization is facing. Accountability refers to all the necessary measurements. Employees must be held accountable and before they can be, job descriptions, expectations, and incentives must be documented. Communications must be clear, precise, and understandable as well as continuous. A safe learning environment must be established where failures are considered necessary steps toward success. Regular reviews to monitor progress and assess direction are required. In the simplest terms of project management, the process steps are: strategize, target, action, and reflect.

A major part of the accountability element is in managing the change. This is actually a continuous and ongoing process to make sure all strategies, objectives, goals, and tactics are aligned. It is very strategic in nature. According to the *Graziadio Business Report* from Pepperdine University, there are six principles to managing change in the business environment.

These six principles are:
1. 'Do no harm.' The best defense against doing no harm is to take a holistic approach.
2. All change involves personal choice. Change is more often resisted than supported in organizations because people rarely are given the chance to understand the reason for the change.

3. The relationship between change and performance is not instantaneous. Change involves time and the opportunity to learn, and learning is often inefficient. So do not expect performance improvement too quickly.
4. Connect change to business strategy. Change should only be pursued in the context of a clear goal, be it personal, group, organizational, or societal.
5. Involvement breeds commitment. The lesson is that involving people in change decisions provides improved estimates of timetables, expectations, and commitment.
6. Any good change effort results in increased capacity to face change in the future.[1]

Sustainability

Once the innovation process has been established, the entrepreneurial small business owner recognizes that it is indeed a process and not a project which comes to an end. On the contrary, the process is a cycle of continuous improvement or more pointedly, sustainable success. It is the basic foundation of the competitive advantage in that it responds to the rapid changes of the business environment. When viewed from the perspective of the total organization, it is the most important value-creating asset of the business.

As was mentioned above, reviews are conducted in the accountability element of the innovation process. This is a good time to consider growth strategies and make sure the business is working effectively and efficiently. Effective work is considered to be the 'things' the business is doing correctly. Efficient work is 'how well' the business performs. The small business owner will keep the organization focused on innovation by examining what and how the business is working.

---

[1] Worley, C. G., Vick, Y. H. (2009). "Leading and Managing Change". Retrieved on 2/15/09 from http://gbr.pepperdine.edu/052/change.html

Additionally, they might consider some of the following:

- How do we decide which markets to focus on?
- Who are our best customers?
- Who are our real competitors?
- What sets us apart?
- How do we turn a brand into a compelling proposition to the marketplace?
- How do we make networks work best for us?

During this cycle of continuous improvement, the innovative entrepreneurial small business owner will connect the unconnected, challenge the status quo, look ahead for new opportunities, and will be seen as the risk taker who is not afraid to try out a new idea. It all begins by looking ahead into the future and from outside of the box.

"The goal of innovation is positive change, to make someone or something better. Innovation leading to increased productivity is the fundamental source of increasing wealth in an economy." [2]

[2] Worley, C. G., Vick, Y. H. (2009). "Leading and Managing Change". Retrieved on 2/15/09 from http://gbr.pepperdine.edu/052/change.html

Effective Relationships

Who are you and who are your team members? What is your preferred method of communicating? How do you see the world and how do you do things differently? Given the same circumstance and task, we all approach the situation from a different perspective. Understanding the differences and similarities that we share with others helps us communicate more effectively and achieve more.

There is more than one right way to handle most situations. A collaborative effort has a higher chance of success than one that is designed by one individual acting by themselves without input from the team. The first step is to develop awareness that we are different and develop ways to recognize the differences. Then we can develop strategic methods to reach out and strengthen our relationships.

Introverted / Extroverted – Are you energized from within and by yourself 'Introverted' or are you energized by associating with others 'Extroverted'? For example, if you are driving home from work and you just miss being in a car accident, would you go home and lay down in a quiet room to rest or would you call your best friend and tell her all about it?

Thinking / Feeling – This preference is the source of much of your analysis and assumptions. 'Thinking' is logical and orderly while 'Feeling' is sensitive to others and considers the not-so-logical impact. For example, if you have been working on a problem and you have the solution, do you say I think I have the answer or I feel that this answer is right?

Sensing / Intuitive – How do you receive information, by your senses or by some internal clock that is hard to identify? For example, if you have to see the hard evidence before you will make up your mind, you are 'Sensing.' If you can imagine the conclusion without seeing all the facts, you are 'Intuitive.'

Our preferences can change depending on the situation but some are usually more dominate. In combination we have defined four relationship types: Action, Energy, Friendship, and Knowledge.

Relationship Types

Action – **Extroverted Thinking / Assertive Action and Direction** - If you attend events and focus on what you want to accomplish, you are extroverted and are highly motivated to get things done. You are action-oriented and always in motion. You are positive, reality-oriented, and assertive. You are single-minded as you focus on results and objectives. You approach others in a direct, authoritative manner, radiating a desire for power and control.

Energy – **Extroverted Feeling / Articulated Vision and Inspiration** - If attending events energizes you, you are strongly extroverted, radiant, and friendly. You are usually positive and concerned with good human relations. You enjoy the company of others and believe that life should be fun. You approach others in a persuasive, democratic manner, radiating a desire for sociability.

Friendship – **Introverted Feeling / One-to-One Relationship and Support** - If you attend events to be with friends, you are an introverted feeler. You focus on values and depth in relationships. You want others to be able to rely on you. You will defend what you value with quiet determination and persistence. You prefer democratic relations that value the individual and are personal in style, radiating a desire for understanding.

Knowledge – **Introverted Thinking / Reflection** - If you attend functions to gain knowledge and gather data, you are introverted and have a desire to know and understand the world around you. You like to think before you act and maintain a detached, objective standpoint. You value independence and intellect. You prefer written communication in order to maintain clarity and precision, and radiate a desire for analysis.

Understanding Differences

How can we begin to recognize and value everyone's differences? Our actions and preferences reflect who we are. We can see actions in others then recognize the differences!

Circle words that describe an individual. The column with the most circles reflects the dominate Relationship Type of that person.

	Action	Energy	Friendship	Knowledge
Energies	• Competitive • Demanding • Determined • Strong-willed • Purposeful • Driver	• Sociable • Dynamic • Demonstrative • Enthusiastic • Persuasive • Expressive	• Caring • Encouraging • Sharing • Patient • Relaxed • Amiable	• Cautious • Precise • Deliberate • Questioning • Formal • Analytical
Verbal	• 'Tell' style • Faster pace • Fills silences • Sounds confident • Responds quickly • Spontaneous	• More emotional • Animated • Casual • Expressive • Asks personal questions	• 'Ask' style • Slower pace • Quieter speech • Thinks first • Diplomatic • Keeps to self	• Controlled • Little emotion • Monotone • Questioning • Critical and blunt • Nit-picker
Inter-action	• Direct • Outgoing • Less patient • Challenges facts • Focus on future	• Relationships • Easy going • Flexible • Friendly and considerate • Small talk • Cooperative	• Indirect • Coordinates • Systematic • Little challenge • Moderate	• Task focus • Punctual • Forthright • Independent • Controlling • Analyses • Evaluates
Body Language	• Leans forward • Full eye contact • Aggressive • Impatient • More gestures • Firm handshake	• Open • Responsive • More expression • Physical contact • Relaxed • Social	• Quiet, reserved • Intermittent eye contact • Gentle handshake • Few gestures • Avoids touch • Reserved	• Detached • Less facial expression • No physical contact • Rigid body • Business-like
Stress	• Become impatient • Increase demands • Increase pressure • Go quicker	• Yell • Scream • Throw things • Take things personally	• Self-destructive thoughts • Deeply-hurt feelings • Ruminating on rights and wrongs	• Withdraw • Try to understand • Split hairs • Wait for certainty • Go quietly

Building Connections

Our objective is to expose you to techniques for networking that may not be intuitive or taught in other settings. Networking is a learned skill that is vital to strategic planning. It is a powerful tool that will increase a business owner's visibility and develop relationships with key contacts. Networking techniques are introduced with the basic premise that to be successful at networking, we share information with others. First we learn how to connect with others to determine not what others can do for us but what we can do to help others.

When we enter a room, we look for ways to make a difference and be of service to others. Every person has valuable information to share and by seeking to help others, we are helped in return. The energy of giving provides a powerful motive to listen carefully to people, waiting for a chance to give assistance. This other-focused giving attitude changes the dynamics of meeting new people and makes us positive, enthusiastic, and genuinely curious about others.

- **Understand** – There are four basic networkers – Those who are energized by networking, those who attend functions to be with friends, those who conduct business, and those who want to learn. Everyone fits in one of those categories most of the time and others sometimes.

- **Ask** – By asking probing questions, discover something interesting about the person you are talking to. Be prepared to introduce your partner to others and share what is interesting about the other person.

- **Listen** – Look for opportunities to help others. Ask, 'What can I do for you?' then listen with the intent to serve.

- **Share** – List who you know and share your resources, i.e., accountants, attorneys, bankers, landscapers. The more you give, the more you will receive. Connect with others and provide them with the information they need.

Networking is really about giving instead of getting. When that is achieved, there is a new level of success. By adopting this powerful attitude, we are immediately eager to meet new people because we know we can make a positive difference in their lives.

Many of the ideas in these exercises are found in *Growing Your Business Through Principled Networking* by Julia Hubbel and published by Ernst and Young LLP.

"Networking is one of three key areas that small businesses should focus on, along with employing technology and developing strategic alliances. Networking is actively making professional relationships, developing and maintaining those relationships, and leveraging them for the benefit of all parties." Jim Blasingame

"The longest journey begins with the first step." Chinese Proverb

It is time to step forward to take networking to the next level and build relationships with key members of your team.

Understand

"Two people see the same object, but they never see it in such a way that the images they receive are absolutely identical." *Psychological Types* by CG Jung. People do not approach networking the same way. There are four groups of people, plus some people feel one way sometimes and another way at other times.

- **Action – You prefer business functions.** You walk in with a list in your head or written down. You walk directly to the first person on your list and complete the task before going to the next person on your list.

- **Energy – You love group functions.** You walk in and notice who is new. You walk up to them and introduce yourself. You explain who you are and what you do so the new person will feel comfortable.

- **Friendship – You prefer small familiar groups.** You walk directly to someone you know. If a stranger asks a question, you only provide a short response until you get to know them better.

- **Knowledge – You prefer a meeting where you learn something new.** You listen carefully to discussions, and then ask detailed questions about any subject that interests you.

While it is easy to identify people who are like you, you may not know how to recognize other types. It is important to adapt and connect to others.

Action – Do's & Don'ts	Energy – Do's & Don'ts
Do • Be direct and to the point • Focus on results and objectives • Be brief, be bright, and be gone **Don't** • Hesitate or dilly-dally • Focus on feelings • Try to take over	**Do** • Be friendly and sociable • Be entertaining and stimulating • Be open and flexible **Don't** • Bore me with details • Tie me down with routine • Ask me to work alone
Friendship – Do's & Don'ts	**Knowledge – Do's & Don'ts**
Do • Be patient and supportive • Slow down and work at my pace • Ask my opinion and give me time to answer **Don't** • Take advantage of my good nature • Push me to make quick decisions • Spring last-minute surprises	**Do** • Be well prepared and thorough • Put things in writing • Let me consider all the details **Don't** • Get too close or hug me • Be flippant on important issues • Change my routine without notice

Identify what type of networker you are. Identify one person for each of the four types. Develop simple approaches (what you plan to do or not do) when you interact with each person on your list.

When attending networking functions, all relationship types can benefit from understanding others, asking questions, listening, then sharing information to help the other person with no strings attached or expectation for something in return.

Ask

Put your attention on the other person, not you! When your focus is on asking the other person about his or her background and opinions, you are making it easy for them to talk. Relax and enjoy the conversation because you do not have to be entertaining or clever. Listen to understand. Pay close attention and listen for intriguing information. Whether approaching a group or one person, come armed with good questions.

Ask open-ended questions and statements which begin with: Who, What, When, Where, Why, and How. Ask for more information or details. Act like a reporter and interview your partner so they will tell you the whole story. You may never find yourself without a conversational partner and your popularity will soar, simply because you are not the one who has to be witty and interesting. Let others shine and as you do, you will be making friends.

No matter whom you are talking to, there is something interesting about that person. Make it a point to find out what that is. Put aside your first impressions. When you can do this, the person's real value can come through. Ask lots of probing questions. If you try hard enough, you will stumble on a truly-interesting story. People are full of surprises. When you focus on what other people have to offer, many opportunities open up for you both.

Ask questions like:

- Tell me about your work. What made you choose it?
- Tell me more about your clients.
- Who do you prefer to work with?
- Why did you choose to live here?
- What is your favorite customer story?

Or ask more personal questions like:
- What was the biggest challenge you have overcome?
- What is the biggest problem you are trying to solve right now?
- What is the funniest thing that has happened to you in your work?

If you do not feel as though you have anything interesting to say about yourself, you are pretty normal. Imagine what happens when you put your attention to finding something interesting about your conversational partner, who often has the same beliefs about himself. When you discover something interesting, you discover it together.

Which questions are the easiest for you to use in a conversation? In the box below, list additional questions you can ask that will help you determine something interesting about others. Go to networking functions with your favorite questions in mind.

Listen

Look for opportunities to help others. Ask, 'What can I do for you?' and then listen with the intent to serve. This attitude takes networking to another level. Look for an opportunity to make a difference in another person's life, whether it is a recommendation for a good restaurant, a referral to your network of friends, a suggestion or an idea, a job opportunity you know about, or an introduction to a friend. Be on the lookout for anything you can offer. Dr. Wayne Dyer says in *You'll See It When You Believe It*, "In a network the purpose is to give power away." In other words, the more you give, the more you get, directly and indirectly. This may go against conventional wisdom, but it works remarkably well when it comes from a genuine service-focused intention.

Searching for a way to be of service requires that you listen at all levels while at the same time thinking about what you have to offer. This places the focus completely on the other person and on what you can give. When you are in a position to give something (and everyone is in that position) you have the power to make someone else's life better. This is exhilarating, and it takes all the pressure off you to be entertaining or witty.

When you give, give without an expectation of getting back. What you offer, whether it is a phone number to a cherished resource or the name of your family chiropractor, it must be given without a demand, implied or stated, that something must be offered in return. Otherwise, it is not a gift. It is coercion. And people can tell the difference.

'No quid pro quo' is the first rule of reciprocity. In *Achieving Success Through Social Capital,* Dr. Wayne Baker explains, "The principle of reciprocity explains why building social capital works: When you use your networks to contribute to others, others contribute to you."

There is an essential difference between offering something freely and offering it with strings, especially when you give something of no value in hopes of getting something of value in return. Here is where you return to your real intention. If your intention is to be of service, and it is an authentic intent, then what you offer will be given freely and without strings. Others sense that and feel free to accept. Does this mean that you should not accept something in return? No. It is important to be clear about what you want and to be open to receiving help. It does mean, however, that your offering does not come with a built-in guilt-load so that the recipient feels that he has to give back. When you always have something to offer others (and your resources are indeed immense) and you are looking to make those resources available, you are very powerful indeed. You have the ability to change people's lives for the better in even the shortest of conversations.

Jot down (maybe on the back of their business card) what the other person needs. You may not have an idea immediately but when you do, you can make the connection.

Share

Identify who you know and share your resources, i.e., accountants, attorneys, bankers, and landscapers. The more you give, the more you will receive.

Your 'social capital' is immense. Social capital is defined as everyone you know in your life and everything all those people have to offer. You do not have to be an expert, just know one. You do not have to have the knowledge, just know where to find it. And it does not have to be work-related. For example, if you have met someone who just moved to town, chances are they are looking for referrals to basic services like a veterinarian or a dentist. If you have good service providers, recommend yours. It takes nothing for you to provide a phone number and an address; chances are they are in your PDA or calendar. It means a great deal to a newcomer to get a recommendation. That is an easy gift to give.

What happens when you enter a networking event with a primary goal of giving your valuable information to others? First of all, you start looking for opportunities to serve. People will be naturally drawn to you because that is the intention you are expressing. You will automatically start asking good questions and listening carefully for ways to give something of value. And when you do, and do it freely, people will be surprised – and very grateful.

As stated earlier, be clear about what you want as well. While you should not ask for something that is clearly out of proportion to the conversation you are having or the relationship you have created, be clear about your needs and let others help you. You might mention that you are starting a company and are looking for potential investors. You can then add that you are wondering if this person has any suggestions about where to start your search. This is less confrontational than asking for help directly. If the person has an interest in your company, he will say so. Otherwise you might get a useful idea or referral which might be just as important. Be willing to be helped, especially if you have been of service first.

Go to your favorite resources and collect their business cards to hand out at networking events. If you do not have cards, bring a pad of Post-it® Notes and an address book with contact information. Be willing to add new resources to your list whenever others share and always be prepared to share your social capital.

Learn to graciously give AND receive to make a lasting difference for you and others you connect with.

A resource chart can be used to identify individuals or organizations that you would be proud to share with others. If you have the information available at networking events, it is easy to provide it to someone who needs a resource. Sharing business cards is great but it is harder to carry a rolodex with you. You can try out different methods and pick the one that works for you.

Resources to Share and Recommend to Others

Name	Company	Type	Address	Phone	e-Mail	Comment

People Strategic Planning

A business needs a complex web of connections to succeed. In its simplest form, relationship management consists of three components: 1) understanding yourself, 2) understanding others, and 3) making connections in a meaningful way.

1. Start with a People S.O.D. Look at your relationships and decide what needs to be done differently. What relationships and roles are important to your success? What are your strengths? What opportunities do you have to improve your relationships? What new approaches will make a difference? What are the dangers if you do not try innovative new ideas and solutions? Your People S.O.D. will begin to trigger ideas that will be used in your 1-PSP.

2. Select two objectives and define S.M.A.R.T. goals that can help you achieve your objectives.

3. List tactics or steps to take in achieving the broader goal.

4. Define what success looks like and list it as the result.

People S.O.D. (Strengths, Opportunities, Dangers)

Strengths	
Opportunities	
Dangers	

People Strategy

Objectives

Goals

Tactics

Results

1-PRC (One-Page Relationship Chart)

Name	Role	Differences	Similarities	Value	Action

Transform ~ Innovate ~ **Stabilize** ~ Grow

Finance Strategy

Strategic Planning			

Stabilize			

Finance Strategy			
S.T.A.R.	**Cash Flow**	**Ratios**	**Financial Process**
Complete S.T.A.R. for Financial Worksheets	Complete the 12-Month Cash Flow	Calculate at least two ratios	Complete the Financial Process identifying at least two goals
Complete Balance Sheet Complete Income Statement Complete Budget Complete Cash Flow	Review existing cash flow statements Project 12-MCF for coming year Use S.T.A.R. to validate assumptions	Calculate Survival Ratio Calculate Growth Ratio Calculate your Z-Score	Utilizing the S.T.A.R. analysis select two goals Define tactics and results for each Complete Financial Strategy section of 1-PSP
S.T.A.R. Analysis	12-MCF	Financial Ratios	1-PSP Financial Strategy

Finance Strategy

The owner of a small business is responsible for the success and survival of the company. The business owner is seldom an economic guru or a highly-educated financial expert. Many owners did not start their business with the intent to make a mark for themselves in the world financial markets or change the course of history through the discovery of a new monetary strategy. The truth is small business owners have a great idea for a new product or service and their passion lies in bringing that idea to market to solve a specific problem or answer a need. When they are successful, it is seldom because they set out to become rich overnight! Many small business owners will quietly confess that the financial side of the business is what they fear the most! They find it confusing, time intensive, and frankly...boring! It comes with its own language and it seems that everyone from accountants, CPAs, and bankers to financial consultants, business analysts, and investment brokers has cornered the market on interpreting it for small business owners.

However, if the small business owner is to survive and become successful, it is in their best interest to understand and control the financial health of their company. Many will tell you that they accomplish this understanding and control through a gut instinct that tells them when the business is heading in the wrong direction or sliding into uncharted territory. The problem with gut instincts is that if one is focused on an immediate need, the instinct can fall second or third to that need. If the gut instinct is on target, by the time the business owner gets around to acting on that instinct, it may be too late. But it does not take a Masters in Finance to understand the basic financial reports for strategic planning and ultimate success for the small business owner. In fact, this is how we can stabilize our business for sustainable success.

What follows is a basic overview of finance for small business owners in order to gain an understanding and a foundation necessary for speaking the language or interpreting the recommendations from the experts.

Continue the S.T.A.R. process by asking yourself key questions as you learn more about your financial statements and the financial condition of your business.

1. **Strategize** – How do the numbers match up with the business strategy? Will the finances support the business focus? Is the business financially sustainable in today's economy based upon the current numbers?

2. **Target** – Are the projections sound or are they based on a best-case financial scenario? Can the business survive a worst-case financial scenario? Do the targets take into consideration a financial reserve should the bottom fall out?

3. **Act** – What steps can be put in place to protect the finances? What moves are necessary to guard against unnecessary spending? Are there income or revenue streams available to be tapped when the primary sources become dry?

4. **Reflect** – How did the business do during the most recent financial period? Did financial changes occur as expected? Were unexpected financial situations managed based upon established back-up plans? What needs to be addressed for the next financial period? Are we moving in a direction to stabilize the business?

Basic Financial Statements

> *"When I want to understand what is happening today, I try to decide what will happen tomorrow; I look back; a page of history is worth a volume of logic." Oliver Wendell Holmes*
>
> Oliver Wendell Holmes (1809-1894) - US author and physician; wrote essay collection "The Autocrat of the Breakfast-Table" 1857, poems "Old Ironsides" "The Chambered Nautilus" "The Deacon's Masterpiece, or, the Wonderful One-Hoss Shay"[3]

Business starts with resources. Those resources may be in the form of cash from the owner, loans from the bank or friends, or the sale of stock for an interest in the business. The resources also may be in the form of real estate, equipment, supplies, fixtures or other items necessary for conducting the business. The business owner is held accountable for obtaining, using, tracking and reporting where those resources are and how they are being utilized. The basic financial statements are one way of accomplishing this task. The balance sheet, income statement, and cash flow statement demonstrate the past use of resources at a given point in time. Most generally, they are prepared on an annual or quarterly basis, although depending on the size of the business they may be prepared as often as monthly. The balance sheet and income statement are examined in greater detail below. The cash flow statement will be discussed later.

At this point, it is also a good idea to be thinking about your 1-PSP (One-Page Strategic Plan). As we learn more about our business's financial condition, we may become aware of certain areas that may need more attention than others. Take note of these areas and put them down as potential objectives in the financial strategic area.

---

[3] BookRags (2009) Oliver Wendell Holmes, Sr. Retrieved on 2/27/2009 from: http://www.bookrags.com/Oliver_Wendell_Holmes,_Sr.

The Balance Sheet

The balance sheet is also known as the statement of financial position. This is appropriate since it represents a summary of the fiscal situation for a business at a specific point in time. The balance sheet consists of three parts: Assets, Liabilities, and Owner's Equity. A mathematical equation exists between the three parts and is stated in different ways lending itself to the document's name...balance sheet. The most common equation is:

$$\text{Assets} = \text{Liabilities} + \text{Owner's Equity}$$

With the Assets listed on the left side of the document, the Liabilities and Owner's Equity are listed on the right side. A total at the bottom of the document will demonstrate that the total amount of assets is exactly equal to the total of liabilities added to the total ownership equity. Therefore, the information 'balances.'

Another way of expressing the equation is:

$$\text{Assets} - \text{Liabilities} = \text{Owner's Equity}$$

This is one way to calculate the sometimes subjective part of the equation, Owner's Equity. However, the balance sheet is generally displayed with the Assets on the left or top of the document and the Liabilities and Owner's Equity on the right or below the Assets.

The contents of the different portions of the balance sheet are listed under each of the three parts. For example, on a small business balance sheet, Assets would be separated between current assets and fixed assets. Current assets might include such items as cash in the bank, accounts receivable, and inventory. Fixed assets are things like real estate and equipment. On the other side of the balance sheet, items listed under Liabilities might include accounts payable, long-term notes and accrued expenses like insurance premiums. Also on this side of the balance sheet are the contributions to the Owner's Equity which as stated above is the difference between the total assets and the total liabilities.

Sample Small Business Balance Sheet[4]

Assets		Liabilities & Owner's Equity		
Cash	$6,600	**Liabilities**		
Accounts Receivable	$6,200	Notes Payable	$30,000	
		Accounts Payable		
		Total Liabilities		$30,000
Tools & Equipment	$25,000	**Owner's Equity**		
		Capital Stock	$7,000	
		Retained Earnings	$800	
		Total Owner's Equity		$7,800
Total	$37,800	*Total*		$37,800

At a glance, the balance sheet can answer the questions of relationship like, 'Does the business own more than it owes?' and 'Is there more short-term debt or long-term debt?' It demonstrates what contributions to the business the owner has supplied. The most important point to remember is that this is still just a snapshot in time. The balance sheet demonstrates what 'was' and not what 'is.' A purchase of expensive equipment tomorrow can change the distribution of the balance sheet.

4 Williams, Jan R.; Susan F. Haka, Mark S. Bettner, Joseph V. Carcello (2008). *Financial & Managerial Accounting*. McGraw-Hill Irwin. pp. 50.

Balance Sheet S.T.A.R.

Locate the latest Balance Sheet for your business or organization. Ask yourself these key questions as you learn more about your financial statements and the financial condition of your business. Rather than try to remember the answers to these and other questions you have about your Balance Sheet, use the space available to make notes. The bottom line is that you want to improve your financial stability and grow your business.

Strategize – How do the numbers match up with the business strategy? Will the finances support the business focus? Is the business financially sustainable in today's economy based upon the current numbers? What objectives and goals will strengthen your financial position?

Target – Are the projections sound or are they based on a best-case financial scenario? Can the business survive a worst-case financial scenario? Do the targets take into consideration a financial reserve should the bottom fall out? What are alternative sources of revenue and options to run efficiently? What are the long-term impacts to the operations?

Act – What steps can be put in place to protect the finances? What moves are necessary to guard against unnecessary spending? Are there income or revenue streams available to be tapped when the primary sources become dry?

Reflect – How did the business do during the most recent financial period? Did financial changes occur as expected? Were unexpected financial situations managed based upon established back-up plans? What considerations need to be addressed for the next financial period? Are we moving in a direction to stabilize the business?

1-PSP – Identify one objective related to the balance sheet on your 1-PSP. This could be as simple as 'Financial Statement Assessment.' (Make a note that the assessment will be specifically related to the balance sheet and this will be addressed in the goal section of the objective.)

The Income Statement

The income statement is sometimes called the Profit and Loss Report because it identifies the profitability of the business during a period of time. An important difference between the balance sheet and the income statement is in the timeframe in which each is reporting. Remember that the balance sheet is a snapshot at a particular point in time, usually a specific date like December 31, 2010. The income statement, on the other hand, is a period of time and is stated as, 'for the three months ending June 30, 2010,' which would mean the period of April 1, 2010, through June 30, 2010. In another example, the income statement might state 'for the month ending January 31, 2010' which in this case would mean the period of January 1, 2010, through January 31, 2010.

The major content of the income statement is important as it lists the revenues, expenses, gains, and losses. The revenues are the proceeds that are realized from the sale of a product or service and sometimes referred to as income. From this amount, expenses are subtracted which leaves the business with a gain or loss for that period of time. The mathematical formula for this document is expressed as:

$$\textbf{Revenues} - \textbf{Expenses} = \textbf{Net Income}$$

Therefore, the income statement measures the profit or loss a business experienced. Generally speaking, the income statement will include the major items of revenues, cost of goods sold, gross profit margin, selling and administrative expense, interest expense, and taxes.

When examining the operating expenses of a business, two items may surface that require a closer look, depreciation and amortization. Depreciation refers to an amount of money that is recognized every year of an item's useful life. For example, we depreciate the cost of equipment over time. If an oven for the baker cost $1000 and is expected to last ten years, then each year, $100 is depreciated for the next ten years.

Depreciation is taken on capital equipment and tangible assets. Amortization also represents a decline in value but relates to only intangible assets such as patents, copyrights, trademarks and goodwill. Like depreciation, amortization allocates the costs of these intangible assets over their useful life.

Additionally, two acronyms are common on the income statement and they are: EBIT and EBITDA. EBIT stands for Earnings Before Interest and Taxes. It is often referred to as Operating Income and is calculated by subtracting Operating Costs from Sales Revenue. The mathematical formula is expressed as:

$$\text{EBIT} = \text{Sales Revenues} - \text{Operating Costs}$$

EBITDA stands for Earnings Before Interest, Taxes, Depreciation, and Amortization. Depreciation and Amortization are not cash expenses even though they are reported as Costs on the income statement. The cash was spent at the time of the purchase. However, it is important to see how much cash a company generates by accounting for the Depreciation and Amortization Costs; that is why EBITDA is calculated.

Success in business is often a measurement of Profit or Net Income. The income statement demonstrates that as revenue goes up, so does Profit. However, when expenses go up, Profit goes down! This means that success is managed by selling as much as possible while keeping the expenses as low as possible.

Caution is advised when preparing and examining the income statement of a business because there are different ways of calculating the information displayed. For example, Depreciation and Inventory can be calculating in at least two different ways that can impact Net Income. An interesting case in point was reported in *The Wall Street Journal* on April 7, 1993, relating to IBM.

"The changes in IBM's accounting practice fell into three broad categories. The first involved revenue recognition and determining when a sale was actually complete. While some high-technology companies wait until a system is installed and running at a customer site, IBM chose to book revenue upon shipment.[5] In some cases, but only when installation at a customer was expected within 30 days, it even booked shipments to its own warehouses as sales. Another revenue issue was how to account for various sales gimmicks that offered customers liberal return policies or price protection refunds if prices later fell. IBM critics contend that full revenue was being booked at shipment, despite evidence that payments received would be less.

"The second category was the treatment of leases. Many of IBM's leases had revenue streams that fell short of GAAP requirements for capital leases. Instead of qualifying as sales when the contract was signed, with all the expected revenue booked at once, they would have to be treated as rentals, with the revenue only booked as payments were received. In an extremely unusual transaction, IBM purchases insurance that guaranteed the value of the computers at the end of the lease. This residual value, when added to the payments from the customer, met the GAAP tests and allowed IBM to recognize the sales immediately.

"Finally, starting in 1984, IBM began to reduce the estimated cost of its retirement plans and to spread the costs of its factories further into the future. Though these changes were fully disclosed in IBM's Financial Statements and were common at other companies, critics maintained they were a shift away from IBM's traditionally conservative accounting."

---

[5] In 1987, the SEC filed suit against another computer manufacturer, Storage Technology Corp., for recognizing revenue when product was shipped rather than installed. The SEC also charged that a major transaction had been backdated in 1983 to turn a loss into a profit. The suit was settled with no admission of wrongdoing.

Sample Income Statement for a fictitious business

Income Statement for Legal Researchers For the year ending December 31, 2008	
Revenues	
Gross Profit (including rental income)	$487,153
Expenses:	
Accounting	$8,425
Advertising	3,521
Bank Fees	398
Employees	93,500
Franchise Fees	15,775
Insurance	9.855
Printing	3.500
Professional Services	9,400
Rent	25,450
Subscriptions	589
Utilities	11,637
Operating Expenses	$182,050
Earnings before interest, taxes, depreciation and amortization (EBITDA)	305,103
Depreciation and Amortization	38,657
Earnings before interest and taxes (EBIT)	$266,446
Interest and Taxes	27,956
NET INCOME	$238,490

Income Statement S.T.A.R.

Locate the latest income statement for your business. Ask yourself these key questions as you learn more about your financial statements and the financial condition of your business. Again, we recommend that you use the space available to make notes. The bottom line is that you want to improve your financial stability and grow your business.

Strategize – How do the numbers match up with the business strategy? Will the finances support the business focus? Is the business financially sustainable in today's economy based upon the current numbers? What objectives and goals will strengthen your financial position?

Target – Are the projections sound or are they based on a best-case financial scenario? Can the business survive a worst-case financial scenario? Do the targets take into consideration a financial reserve should the bottom fall out? What are alternative sources of revenue and options to run efficiently? What are the long-term impacts to the operations?

Act – What steps can be put in place to protect the finances? What moves are necessary to guard against unnecessary spending? Are there income or revenue streams available to be tapped when the primary sources become dry?

```

```

Reflect – How did the business do during the most recent financial period? Did financial changes occur as expected? Were unexpected financial situations managed based upon established back-up plans? What considerations need to be addressed for the next financial period? Are we moving in a direction to stabilize the business?

```

```

1-PSP – Identify one objective related to the income statement on your 1-PSP. This could be as simple as 'Financial Statement Assessment.' (Make a note that the assessment will be specifically related to the income statement and this will be addressed in the goal section of the objective.)

```

```

Budgets

> *"A budget tells us what we can't afford, but it doesn't keep us from buying it."* William Feather
>
> William Feather (1889 – 1981) was an American publisher and author, based in Cleveland, Ohio.[6]

Budgets or the budgeting process practiced by small businesses is often referred to as a necessary evil and brings about a series of low groans from those individuals assigned to the task. While many tasks listed under the accounting or financial umbrella are viewed as boring, the budget exercise, when properly explained, can become one of the most interesting and exciting aspects of any small business. Previously, it was noted that the balance sheet and income statements are documents reflecting a business at a specific point in time. Said another way, these are historical references. The budget, on the other hand, is a document of the current situation. It measures what is expected to be spent against what was actually spent.

The purpose of the small business budget is two-fold. First, it is a forecast of the income and expenses expected based on the business plan. Second, it is a documented account of how the business performed based on that forecast. As such, the budget is a control tool for managing the day-to-day activities of the business.

Additionally, to be more effective, and wherever possible, consider a budget that:

a) Reflects the reality of the business - Line items should identify the needs, wants, and nice-to-haves of the business, in that order.
b) Connects accurately from one period to the next - Positive and negative balances of a prior period should be reflected in the current period.
c) Tracks all of the funds - Use zero-based budgeting to allocate every item.

---

[6] Wikipedia. William A. Feather http://en.wikipedia.org/wiki/William_Feather

A small business budget is generally created once a year and reviewed monthly, quarterly, or even semi-annually. Quite often the budget is reviewed first when financial decisions are required as a means of assessing the business's current fiscal position. Management, and sometimes employees, are granted limits on expenditures without seeking prior approval based on the portions of the business budget they control.

Budgets are often a measure of performance, both for a company and for the management team. This can be a true balancing act that should not be taken lightly. When managers feel they are constrained by a budget they had no input into, they will be prone to manipulate the results, putting themselves in the best light. The better approach is allowing management and employees a voice in creating the budget. Performance can be measured not only on how well they adhere to the budget but also in how well they adjust to changes in the business and apply those changes appropriately to the budget. In this way, the budget becomes a living document that works towards the fundamental success and survival of the business.

The small business budget generally identifies expected income and expense amounts for a specified line item in one column and the corresponding actual amounts in the next column. Sometimes a third column is created that displays the difference between the two amounts. This is called the variance. The variance may be a positive number or a negative number depicting whether a particular line item is over/under budget.

A popular form of budgeting is called the 'zero-based budget' which means that every dollar of income is identified with a specific expense causing the sum of incomes to be equal to the sum of expenses. Put another way, the total amount of income minus the total amount of expense equals zero. The mathematical formula for this document would be:

$$\text{Total Income} - \text{Total Expense} = 0$$

There are a variety of sub-types of budgets that can be used by a small business.

These include but are not limited to:

- Sales budget
- Inventory budget
- Production budget
- Cash budget
- Marketing budget
- Project budget

At the end of the day, the budget is the business document that tells the small business owner whether they are going in the direction they intended. It puts the small business owner in control of the finances rather than the finances controlling the business. Most of all, it allows for goals to be met and a financial crisis to be averted; that means that the business owner can get a good night's sleep!

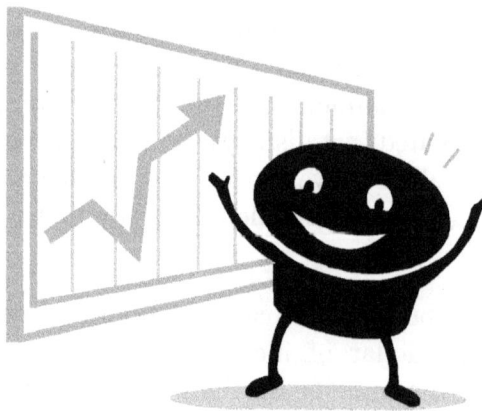

Sample Budget for a small business

Widget Manufacturing Company			
Budget			
January 1, 2009 to December 31, 2009			
Category	**Actual**	**Budget**	**Variance** (over) / under
Inflows			
Net Sales	$384,500	$300,000	($84,500)
Cost of Goods			
Merchandise Inventory, January 1	160,000	160,000	0
Purchases	120,000	90,000	(30,000)
Freight charges	2,500	2,000	(500)
Total Merchandise Handled	282,500	252,000	(30,500)
Less Inventory, December 31	100,000	120,000	20,000
Cost of Goods Sold	182,500	132,000	(50,500)
Gross Profit	202,000	168,000	(34,000)
Interest Income	500	700	200
Total Income	**202,500**	**168,700**	(33,800)
Expenses			
Salaries	68,250	45,000	(23,250)
Utilities	5,800	4,500	(1,300)
Rent	23,000	23,000	0
Office Supplies	2,250	3,000	750
Insurance	3,900	3,900	0
Advertising	8,650	9,000	350
Telephone	2,700	2,300	(400)
Travel and Entertainment	2,550	2,000	(550)
Dues & Subscriptions	1,100	1,000	(100)
Interest Paid	2,140	2,500	360
Repairs & Maintenance	1,250	1,000	(250)
Taxes & Licenses	11,700	10,000	(1,700)
Total Expenses	**133,290**	**106,850**	(26,440)
Net Income	**$69,210**	**$61,850**	($7,360)

Cash Flow Management

> *"Increased borrowing must be matched by increased ability to repay. Otherwise we aren't expanding the economy, we're merely puffing it up."*
> Henry C. Alexander
>
> Henry C. Alexander (1902 – 1969) Alexander changed the way in which the Morgan Bank did business. Before Alexander, the Morgan Bank did not solicit business. Alexander used greater aggressiveness in the development of new business by training a new generation of employees, known as "bird dogs," to pursue business that had previously come in by itself. His greatest achievement was the merger of JP Morgan with the Guaranty Bank. Prior to the merger, Alexander served as the chief executive of JP Morgan & Company from 1950-1959.[7]

Cash flow management has been described as many things including the process of monitoring, analyzing, and dealing with the small business cash flows. According to a December 11, 2003, article in *Growing Your Business*, "...cash flow management means delaying outlays of cash as long as possible while encouraging anyone who owes you money to pay it as rapidly as possible."[8] This is certainly true during a down economy, but also holds true for any small business owner with their sights set on growing their business. While growth will be easier for any business with a zero-to-low-debt ratio, many small business owners might well be advised to manage their company finances through an effective cash flow plan.

Planning and managing cash flow helps the small business owner prepare, monitor, and execute good business decisions based on the money coming in and going out of the business. One way to accomplish the task is to pay close attention to four basic areas: 1) Cash Flow Plan; 2) Receivables; 3) Payables; and 4) Murphy.

---

[7] Harvard Business School Leadership Database. (2009). "Henry C. Alexander". Retrieved on 2/27/2009 from: http://www.hbs.edu/leadership/database/leaders/henry_c_alexander.html

[8] Growing Your Business (December 11, 2003). "How To Better Manage Your Cash Flow". Entreprenuer.com. Retrieved 3/4/2008 from:
http://www.entrepreneur.com/money/moneymanagement/managingcashflow/article66008.html

Cash Flow Plan

A cash flow plan is much like a budget but generally is viewed over a greater period of time and demonstrates anticipated highs and lows of the cash required to run the business. It is a forward or future view of the anticipated movement of funds in a business.

Information is gathered from all parts of the business to validate the numbers on the plan. Notes or references to documents should be included, especially when information provided is not generally well known or is an infrequent occurrence. Some information will be easily documented such as fixed payables and receivables. Other data will be more subjective like the varied costs of operations or anticipated sales revenues. It is very important that the subjective data be as accurate as possible or there is no value in creating the cash flow plan.

Many experts consider the cash flow plan to be as important to a business as their strategic plan and mission statement. When preparing the cash flow plan, special attention is focused on funds coming into and going out of a business over a future period of time. Additionally, this is where the focus is placed on the probability of unforeseen occurrences.

Receivables

Accounts receivable is one of those items that really looks good on paper, but masks an incredible power to bring a business to its knees or worse! The term 'Cash is King' goes a long way to loosen the grip and put the power to grow back in the hands of the small business owner. Businesses that run on cash sales or credit cards only tend to enjoy more opportunities for growth, especially when paired with a well-established cash flow plan. For small businesses that are suffering from slow-paying customers, consider cutting losses by offering a discount on balances if paid immediately. Of course, it goes without saying that a slow-paying customer's credit should be cut off and buying limited to cash only.

Receivables should be managed tightly so put them 'Under the Microscope.' This means that credit customers should be billed quickly, offered discounts for early payment, accrue penalties from late payment, and should not be allowed to go indefinitely without paying. This includes their ability to continue purchasing when past purchases have over-due payments! Collection services may be an alternative, but sometimes it is best to take a write-off and cancel the customer's credit.

In addition to examining receivables, check on old inventory. Inventory which is not moving, and has been paid for in full, is still costing the company in terms of space and possibly shelf-life. Identify ways to move the inventory and bring cash into your business. Many small business owners utilize 'end-of-year' sales or off-season price reductions to attract cost-conscience customers.

Payables

Just as receivables must be managed, so must the business's payables. However, this is the flip side of the situation and the emphasis is 'Control the Payables'!

Examine the terms of the payables to vendors. It may be beneficial to take advantage of discounts for cash payments especially where the item has been ordered and payment received from customers. Sometimes, when supplies or materials have been purchased but are still 'works-in-process,' payment terms should not be paid until due. In this case, the cash of the business is working longer and harder for the small business owner than for the vendor. Electronic payments to vendors should be made at the last possible day for the same reason. It is important to remember, payments should always be on time, not late. This keeps the small business owner in good standing; and if necessary in the future, provides leverage for requesting extensions.

Murphy

Have you ever heard the saying, 'Murphy's Law'? It is a fact of life that unexpected things happen at the most inopportune times. The cash flow plan can be utilized as a strategic instrument to counteract this phenomenon. By accruing for 'Murphy,' funds will be available to offset the unexpected.

Even if the unexpected event requires more than the funds accrued, the small business owner is in a better position by having more alternatives. For example, if no funds have been accrued, the unexpected event may force the cutting of employees, the sale of a business line, or even the close of the business. On the other hand, with some accrued funds, the business owner may be able to approach a family member, friend, banker, or investor with a short-term solution based on their ability to provide a portion of the cash required instead of a physical asset put up as collateral. In tough times, a business owner that demonstrates their ability to plan for the unexpected will always be more credit worthy than one that runs a business without a back-up plan.

The Cash Flow Statement

Cash Flow Statement Steve's Motor Repair and Sales For Year Ended December 31, 2009	
Cash Flow From Operations	
Net Earnings	3,500,000
Additions to Cash	
Depreciation	35,000
Decrease in Accounts Receivable	47,000
Increase in Accounts Payable	43,000
Increase in Taxes Payable	9,650
Subtractions From Cash	
Increase in Inventory	35,000
Net Cash from Operations	3,599,650
Cash Flow from Investing	
Equipment	(670,000)
Cash Flow from Financing	
Notes Payable	35,200
Cash Flow for Year Ended December 31, 2009	2,964,850

As mentioned earlier, the cash flow statement is one of the basic financial statements and as such provides a historic view of the business's cash flow. When examining the format of the cash flow statement it is important to understand that it is different from the other financial statements in that it does not include the amount of future cash that has been recorded on credit. For example, cash sales and credit sales are both on the balance sheet and income statement.

The cash flow statement looks at three specific areas of the business where the cash is generated. Specifically, it identifies operations, investing, and financing. Changes are reflected based on whether the cash is flowing in or out of the business. Operations are related to the products and/or services of the business. Investing typically deals with equipment, assets, and investment opportunities. The financing portion is associated with debts, loans, and dividends.

12-Month Cash Flow S.T.A.R.

In this exercise, you are going to create your own 12-month cash flow plan. You may use the template at the end of this section. Research your own business records and locate the information required. Once you have the data completed, answer the following questions:

Refer to the S.T.A.R. process and apply the key questions below to this financial document.

Strategize – How do the numbers match up with the business strategy? Will the finances support the business focus? Is the business financially sustainable in today's economy based upon the current numbers? What objectives and goals will strengthen your financial position?

Target – Are the projections sound or are they based on a best-case financial scenario? Can the business survive a worst-case financial scenario? Do the targets take into consideration a financial reserve should the bottom fall out? What are alternative sources of revenue and options to run efficiently? What are the long-term impacts to the operations?

SMALL BUSINESS STRATEGIC PLANNING

Act – What steps can be put in place to protect the finances? What moves are necessary to guard against unnecessary spending? Are there income or revenue streams available to be tapped when the primary sources become dry?

Reflect – How did the business do during the most recent financial period? Did financial changes occur as expected? Were unexpected financial situations managed based upon established back-up plans? What considerations need to be addressed for the next financial period? Are we moving in a direction to stabilize the business?

1-PSP – Identify one objective related to the cash flow on your 1-PSP. This could be as simple as 'Financial Statement Assessment.' (Make a note that the assessment will be specifically related to the cash flow and this will be addressed in the goal section of the objective.)

Checks and Balances

> *"What has not been examined impartially has not been well examined. Skepticism is therefore the first step toward truth." Denis Diderot*
>
> Denis Diderot (1713 – 1784) French man of letters and philosopher who, from 1745 to 1772, served as chief editor of the *Encyclopédie*, one of the principal works of the Age of Enlightenment.[9]

When checks and balances are in place, a small business owner can feel more at ease that the business is running as intended. However, control over those checks and balances must be observed on a regular basis, i.e., audits and verifications. The Sarbanes-Oxley Act of 2002 identified the importance of internal financial controls in minimizing fraud and abuse.

The intent of financial controls is to ensure timely information whether that information comes from manual or automated systems. The basis of internal financial controls is the accuracy of transactions. An internal control system consists of several activities, techniques and concepts but is not complex or difficult to implement. The small business owner will rest easier when steps have been taken to avoid predictable pitfalls.

The basic model for protecting a business through internal controls would include but is not necessarily limited to the following: Segregation of Duties, Physical Controls, Reconciliations, Self-Interest, Control Numbers, Delegation of Authority, Maintaining Controls, and Audits.

---

[9] Wikipedia (2009). Denis Diderot. Retrieved on 2/26/2009 from: http://en.wikipedia.org/wiki/Dennis_Diderot

Segregation of Duties

Segregation of Duties means to separate authorizations, custody, and record-keeping tasks in order to limit the amount of risk posed by fraud or error. For example, someone who is responsible for writing checks should not be able to sign the check or reconcile the bank statements. Customer payments which are received in the mail should go to the bank or be opened and totaled by someone different than the person responsible for posting payments to the journals or computer system.

Physical Controls

Physical Control means tight control for access to business assets. The most common example is locking up the checkbook in a safe with only one or two individuals having the key or combination to retrieve it. Another good example is inventory. Inventory is generally placed in a locked or controlled environment with log sheets showing who retrieved what, when, and how much. Quite often the log will identify not only the persons receiving the materials but also the persons who authorized the distribution of the inventory from the storage area.

Generally, most small businesses also maintain identifying marks, labels, or stickers on major business assets like computer systems, vehicles, equipment, and office furniture. In recent years, more small businesses are protecting assets with security systems which might include cameras, armed guards, and audible alarms.

Reconciliations

Reconciliations are important for internal financial controls. Not only do they provide timely and accurate information to identify any potential errors, but the data are often necessary for business decisions. The growth, success, and survival of any small business are dependent upon having them.

Examples of reconciliations include:

- Monthly bank statements reconciled with the checkbook
- Accounts payable and receivable ledger balances reconciled to detailed aging reports
- Inventory of supplies and materials reconciled to shipping receipts
- Fixed assets reconciled to depreciation schedules
- Vendor payable balances reconciled to statements received
- Long-term notes or accrued liabilities journals reconciled against billings and statements.

Generally, these items are managed through the monthly close process and records of the close maintained in a separate locked area.

Self-Interest

Self-interest refers to individuals acting in their own best interest. For example, few people are likely to alert the clerk at the register if an item is omitted from their bill. However, those same people will be the first to inform a merchant that they have been charged for an item they did not order. This concept is important to recognize because in the area of financial controls it is an important motivator. If an inventory clerk's pay is tied to shortages and overages in inventory, they are going to be more meticulous in overseeing the accuracy of what moves in and out of inventory. Another example of how well this concept is recognized is when employees are not paid for business expenses they incur until providing documented receipts.

Control Numbers

Control numbers assure that transactions are not lost or do not slip through cracks. It is also a very helpful way of cross-referencing the transactions. Many automated accounting systems provide this functionality as a way of tracking items through various accounting components. Control numbers and logs are one of the most useful ways of reconciling differences, finding the source of errors, and recognizing how to correct process problems. The most common example of control numbers and logs is checks and the checkbook register. Another common use is invoice numbers.

Delegation of Authority

Delegation of authority is another good financial control measure. This means that there is a clearly-stated policy in place which identifies who has authority to approve and perform specific actions. It is much like segregation of duties, but generally refers to approval on dollar amounts. For example, first-line supervisors may have the authority to approve supply orders up to $500. Managers may have authority to approve various purchasing decisions up to $5,000. Amounts over $5,000 may require an officer and owner's approval based on the item. Keep in mind that authorization levels should include non-cash items such as purchase returns to avoid bottle-necks in the process.

Maintaining Controls

It is important that the processes and control for financial systems have the utmost integrity. If a system is perceived to be faulty, individuals will begin to work around the system; this opens the door to various kinds of errors and especially fraud. Maintaining controls means validating and verifying that the systems are working as designed and assuring that employees are trained and updated on changes in the process. The biggest mistake small businesses make is thinking that short-cuts can be taken on controls and not following the processes established. The fallacy of this reasoning leads to more work in identifying errors on the back end. The fact is that the more attention and planning that goes into controlling the systems on the front end, ultimately speeds up the process for delivering timely and accurate data.

Audits

Audits are the cornerstone of internal financial controls. They are not to be confused with searching for fraud, but they are used for providing assurance that the data delivered via the financial system is accurate. When fraud is suspected, experts, such as forensic accountants, should be contacted to address the issues. Standard audits of systems may be conducted at routine intervals by CPAs and by internal personnel. Audits are reviewed for recommendations and actions to be implemented where appropriate.

As identified above, internal controls are the basis for timely and accurate financial reporting. Additionally, these controls guard against loss and errors. While not all controls are cost-effective, the small business owner must weigh the risks with the rewards and judge for themselves where their comfort level exists. Sources for evaluating the appropriate controls for any business can be found by asking the experts: CPAs, information technology security analysts, attorneys, bankers, and insurance agents.

Financial Management

Financial Management is the process by which business owners and managers maximize the value of their business. Throughout this section, attention has been paid to simplifying much of the complex nature of this process. In addition to the methods described previously, Financial Management can also be examined through the use of several Financial Ratios. At the end of this section there is a list of several Financial Ratios comparing a fictitious company to its industry average. This is a valuable resource for identifying, calculating, and understanding the implications of ratios reviewed by financial institutions.

For our purposes in this discussion, we want to look at only two specific ratios. The first ratio is easy to calculate and easy to understand. It can be the first sign of trouble in the business so we want to keep an eye on it! In the financial industry it is called the 'Liquidity Ratio' but we call it our 'Survival Ratio'!

Here is the formula:

Survival = Current Assets / Current Liabilities

Notice the Current Assets and Current Liabilities are both found on the Balance Sheet. To understand the ratio, we need to recognize that when a business is starting to have financial trouble, they may start paying bills slowly. When they do, current liabilities start going up faster than current assets. As this happens, the survival ratio goes DOWN↓. So a low ratio (when compared to the previous period or your industry average) can indicate a business in trouble. For strategic planning, aim to keep this ratio HIGH↑!

The second ratio is also easy to calculate and understand. It measures how well or efficiently we are managing the business. This is our report card so we want to keep a sharp eye on it, as well! In the financial industry it is called the 'Debt Ratio' but we call it our 'Growth Ratio'! Here is the formula:

Growth = Total Debt / Total Assets

Again, both Total Debt and Total Assets are found on the Balance Sheet. This ratio tells us how much funding for the business is being provided by creditors. If the business is carrying a high amount of debt, it could make it difficult to obtain additional funding and limit our ability to grow the business! However, if the business is running on low debt, it demonstrates the ability to fund growth through operations. We are managing through efficient practices and get an "A" on our report card! So, a low ratio (when compared to the previous period or your industry average) indicates a well-run operation that is growing!

A final measure of a company's solvency might be calculated using the Z-score. This mathematical equation was created by Edward Altman in the early 1960s. By entering in the required values, the calculator will produce the probability of the business failing. See pages 97 - 98 for further details.

SUMMARY

Interpreting and understanding the financial situation of a small business does not need to be a cumbersome exercise. By paying attention to the financial health of the business itself, survival, success, and growth can be attained and sustained. In this way we have learned to stabilize our business. Incorporating the S.T.A.R. process into your financial processes will add value and strength to your business. Remember that financial statements are a must and include the balance sheet, income statement, and cash flow statement. Budgets can be exciting and help the business run smoother. The cash flow plan anticipates the future and guards against the unexpected. Finally, the process of financial management through the use of a variety of ratios will help the small business owner identify their financial health and lead them in making sound business decisions.

As we wrap up the financial area of this forum, remember that a healthy review of your financial strengths, opportunities, and dangers (S.O.D.) is in order. These environmental elements along with the financial statements and financial tools are all important pieces to a solid financial foundation for the business. They require us to stay continuously aware of our condition. Therefore, in order to be successful, it is a must that our 1-PSP captures our financial strategy and we implement appropriate action plans.

Glossary[10]

Amortization	The systematic allocation of the discount, premium, or issue costs of a bond to expense over the life of the bond; the systematic allocation of an intangible asset to expense over a certain period of time; the systematic reduction of a loan's principal balance through equal payment amounts which cover interest & principal repayment.
Assets	Things that are resources owned by a company and which have future economic value that can be measured and can be expressed in dollars. Examples include cash, investments, accounts receivable, inventory, supplies, land, buildings, equipment, and vehicles. Assets are reported on the balance sheet usually at cost or lower. Assets are also part of the accounting equation: Assets = Liabilities + Owner's (Stockholders') Equity. Some valuable items that cannot be measured and expressed in dollars include the company's outstanding reputation, its customer base, the value of successful consumer brands, and its management team. As a result these items are not reported among the assets appearing on the balance sheet.
Audit	An examination of a company's financial statements by an independent accountant. The result is a signed opinion of whether the statements fairly reflect the company's financial results and position.
Balance Sheet	One of the main financial statements. The balance sheet reports the assets, liabilities, and owner's (stockholders') equity at a specific point in time, such as December 31. The balance sheet is also referred to as the Statement of Financial Position.

---

[10]Comprised from:

Low, Robert (2004), Accounting and Finance for Small Business Made Easy. Madison, Wisconsin:CWL Publishing Enterprises, Inc.; AccountingCoach.com (2009). Accounting Terms. Retrieved 3/5/2009 from: http://www.accountingcoach.com/accounting-terms/accounting-dictionary/index.html; and EnviroTech Financial, Inc. (2009) Financial Terms. Retrieved 3/5/2009 from: http://www.etfinancial.com/financialterms.htm

Budget	A planned level of expenditures, usually at a fairly detailed level. A company may plan and maintain a budget on either an accrual or a cash basis.
Cash Flow Management	The process of monitoring, analyzing, and adjusting your business's cash flows.
Cash Flow Statement	One of the main financial statements (along with the income statement and balance sheet). The statement of cash flows reports the sources and uses of cash by operating activities, investing activities, financing activities, and certain supplemental information for the period specified in the heading of the statement.
Current Assets	Cash and other resources that are expected to turn to cash or to be used up within one year of the balance sheet date. If a company's operating cycle is longer than one year, an item is a current asset if it will turn to cash or be used up within the operating cycle. Current assets are presented in the order of liquidity, i.e., cash, temporary investments, accounts receivable, inventory, supplies, prepaid insurance.
Current Liabilities	Obligations due within one year of the balance sheet date. If a company's operating cycle is longer than one year, an item is a current liability if it is due within the operating cycle. Another condition is that the item will use cash or it will create another current liability. This means that if a bond payable is due within one year of the balance sheet date, but the bond will be retired by a bond sinking fund (a long-term restricted asset) the bond will not be reported as a current liability.
Depreciation	The systematic allocation of the cost of an asset from the balance sheet to Depreciation Expense on the income statement over the useful life of the asset. The depreciation journal entry includes a debit to Depreciation Expense and a credit to Accumulated Depreciation, a contra asset account. The purpose is to allocate the cost to expense in order to comply with the matching principle. It is not intended to be a valuation process. In other words, the amount allocated to expense is not indicative of the economic value being consumed. Similarly, the amount not yet allocated is not an indication of its current market value.

Expenses	Costs that are matched with revenues on the income statement. For example, Cost of Goods Sold is an expense caused by Sales. Insurance Expense, Wages Expense, Advertising Expense, Interest Expense are expenses matched with the period of time in the heading of the income statement. Under the accrual basis of accounting, the matching is NOT based on the date that the expenses are paid.
	Expenses associated with the main activity of the business are referred to as operating expenses. Expenses associated with a peripheral activity are non-operating or other expenses. For example, a retailer's interest expense is a non-operating expense. A bank's interest expense is an operating expense.
	Generally, expenses are debited to a specific expense account and the normal balance of an expense account is a debit balance. When an expense account is debited, the account credited might be Cash, Accounts Payable, or Prepaid Expense depending on whether cash was paid at the time of the expense, the payment will be made after the expense was incurred, or the expense was paid in advance.
Fixed Assets	A term used when referring to property, plant, and equipment. Fixed assets other than land are depreciated.
Income Statement	One of the main financial statements (along with the balance sheet, the statement of cash flows, and the statement of stockholders' equity). The income statement is also referred to as the profit and loss statement, P&L, statement of income, and the statement of operations. The income statement reports the revenues, gains, expenses, losses, net income and other totals for the period of time shown in the heading of the statement. If a company's stock is publicly traded, earnings per share must appear on the face of the income statement.
Liabilities	Obligations of a company or organization. Amounts owed to lenders and suppliers. Liabilities often have the word 'payable' in the account title. Liabilities also include amounts received in advance for a future sale or for a future service to be performed.
Loss	The result of the sale of an asset for less than its carrying amount; the write-down of assets; the net result of expenses exceeding revenues.

Owner's Equity	The book value of a company equal to the recorded amounts of assets minus the recorded amounts of liabilities.
Profit	Total revenues minus total expenses, including taxes and depreciation, for a specified time.
Revenues	Fees earned from providing services and the amounts of merchandise sold. Under the accrual basis of accounting, revenues are recorded at the time of delivering the service or the merchandise, even if cash is not received at the time of delivery. Often the term *income* is used instead of revenues. Examples of revenue accounts include: Sales, Service Revenues, Fees Earned, Interest Revenue, and Interest Income. Revenue accounts are *credited* when services are performed / billed and therefore will usually have credit balances. At the time that a revenue account is credited, the account debited might be Cash, Accounts Receivable, or Unearned Revenue depending if cash was received at the time of the service, if the customer was billed at the time of the service and will pay later, or if the customer had paid in advance of the service being performed. If the revenues earned are a main activity of the business, they are considered to be operating revenues. If the revenues come from a secondary activity, they are considered to be non-operating revenues. For example, interest earned by a manufacturer on its investments is a non-operating revenue. Interest earned by a bank is considered to be part of operating revenues.
Variance	A term used with standard costs to report a difference between actual costs and standard costs.

Sample of Financial Ratios Compared to Industry Average for a Fictitious Company[11]

Ratio	Formula	Calculation	Ratio	Industry Average	Comment
Liquidity					
Current	Current Assets / Current Liabilities	$1,000 / $310	=3.2x	4.2x	Poor
Quick	Current Assets − Inventories / Current Liabilities	$384 / $310	=1.2x	2.2x	Poor
Asset Management					
Inventory Turnover	Sales / Inventories	$3,000 / $615	=4.9x	10.9X	Poor
Days Sales Outstanding (DSO)	Receivables / Annual Sales / 365	$375 / $8.21	=46 days	36 days	Poor
Fixed Assets Turnover	Sales / Net Fixed Assets	$3,000 / $1,000	=3.0x	2.8x	OK
Total Assets Turnover	Sales / Total Assets	$3,000 / $2,000	=1.5x	1.8x	Somewhat low
Debt Management					
Total Debt to Total Assets	Total Debt / Total Assets	$1,060 / $2,000	=53.0%	40.0%	High (risky)
Times-Interest-Earned (TIE)	Earnings Before Interest and Taxes (EBIT) / Interest Charges	$283 / $88	=3.2x	6.0x	Low (risky)
EBITDA Coverage	EBITDA + Lease payments / Interest+Principal Payments+Lease Payments	$411 / $136	=3.0x	4.3x	Low (risky)

[11]Brigham, E. F., Houston, J. F. (2007), Fundamentals of Financial Management, Eleventh Edition. Mason, OH: Thompson South-Western. P.119.

Ratio	Formula	Calculation	Ratio	Industry Average	Comment
Profitability					
Profit Margin on Sales	Net Income / Sales	$117 / $3,000	-3.9%	5.0%	Poor
Return on Total Assets (ROA)	Net Income / Total Assets	$117 / $2,000	-5.9%	9.0%	Poor
Basic Earning Power (BEP)	Earnings Before Interest and Taxes (EBIT) / Total Assets	$283 / $2,000	- 14.2%	18.0%	Poor
Return on Common Equity (ROE)	Net Income / Common Equity	$117 / $940	- 12.5%	15.0%	Poor
Market Value					
Price / Earnings (P/E)	Price per Share / Earnings per Share	$23 / $2.35	-9.8x	11.3x	Low
Price /Cash Flow	Price per Share / Cash Flow per Share	$23 / $4.35	-5.3X	5.4X	Low
Market / Book (M/B)	Market Price per Share / Book Value per Share	$23 / $18.80	-1.2x	1.7x	Low

Measuring a Company's 'Fiscal-Fitness': Altman Z-Score

In the early 60s Edward Altman, using Multiple Discriminate Analysis, combined a set of five financial ratios to come up with the Altman Z-Score. This score uses statistical techniques to predict a company's probability of failure using the following eight variables from a company's financial statements.

Income Statement:
        Earnings Before Interest & Taxes (EBIT) and Net Sales
Balance Sheet:
        Total Assets, Market Value of Equity, Total Liabilities,
        Current Assets, Current Liabilities, and Retained Earnings

Follow this link to access the Altman Z Score Calculator: www.creditguru.com/CalcAltZ.shtml.

The five financial ratios in the Altman Z-Score and their respective weight factor are as follows:

	Ratio	Weight	
A	EBIT / Total Assets	x. 3.3	-4 to +8.0
B	Net Sales / Total Assets	x 0.999	-4 to +8.0
C	Market Value of Equity / Total Liabilities	x 0.6	-4 to +8.0
D	Working Capital / Total Assets	x 1.2	-4 to +8.0
E	Retained Earnings / Total Assets	x 1.4	-4 to +8.0

These ratios are multiplied by the weight above, and then the results are added together.

Z-Score = A x 3.3 + B x 0.99 + C x 0.6 + D x 1.2 + E x 1.4

The Interpretation of Z Scores	
Above 3.0	The company is safe based on these financial figures only.
Between 2.7 and 3.0	On Alert. This zone is an area where one should exercise caution.
Between 1.8 and 2.7	Good chances of the company going bankrupt within 2 years of operations from the date of financial figures given.
Below 1.8	Probability of financial embarrassment is very high.

Follow this link to access the Altman Z Score Calculator:
www.creditguru.com/CalcAltZ.shtml

Internal Control Questionnaire for Cash Disbursements[12]

Internal controls can provide protection from loss and errors. Use the following Questionnaire to determine if you have established effective internal controls in the area of cash disbursements.

Accessibility or Safeguarding

Physical controls and restricted access are important control tools. Review this section to see if your procedures can use improvement.

Yes	No	
		Are all payments made by check or other negotiable instruments?
		Are checks made payable to specific payees?
		Are your checks pre-numbered and used in sequence?
		Are voided, special or mutilated checks saved and filed?
		Does someone check the sequence of checks periodically?
		Do you store unused checks in a restricted area in the possession of a specified person?
		Are checks made of protective paper?
		Is a check protector used?
		If you use facsimile plates or similar devices for check signatures, have you identified who is to have custody and use of the plates?
		Do you keep facsimile plates in a restricted, secure place apart from blank check stock? Are the plates used only in the presence of the person designated as responsible?

---

[12]Low, Robert (2004), Accounting and Finance for Small Business Made Easy. Madison, Wisconsin: CWL Publishing Enterprises, Inc. pp. 286-289.

Separation of Duties

Maintaining a distinct separation of duties is one of the most important practices you can establish for controlling unauthorized expenditures, theft, and errors.

Yes	No	
		Are checks prepared by persons other than those with voucher approval authority?
		Is the person who prepares checks independent of purchasing and receiving functions?
		Are checks signed by persons other than those preparing or having approval authority?
		Are authorized signatures limited to employees having no access to accounting records, cash receipts, or petty cash funds?
		Is there a dollar limit at which all checks must be countersigned?
		Are bank reconciliations prepared monthly by an employee who does not sign checks, records cash transactions or have access to cash?
		Does this person receive the bank statement unopened?

Record corrective actions you need to take.

Processing and Recording

Review the questions below to check whether your Processing and Recording procedures provide enough checks and balances to detect incorrect transactions.

Yes	No	
		Are all regular disbursements that you make by checks prepared and based on adequate and approved documentation?
		Does the person who signs checks verify whether the amounts are approved and have adequate documentation?
		Do you pay only against original invoices & not against statements or photocopies?
		Do you mark invoices after payment & check for duplicate numbers to avoid paying twice?
		Are only complete checks – not blank – ever signed?
		After signing, are all checks recorded in a cash disbursement record that gives enough detail to allow accurate summarizing and posting?
		Are actual disbursements periodically compared with forecasted disbursements and larger or unusual variances investigated and accounted for?

What processes or procedures do you need to evaluate and rewrite?

Finance Strategic Planning

If the small business owner is to survive and become successful, it is in their best interest to understand and control the financial health of their company.

1. Start with a Finance S.O.D. Look at your finances. Decide what needs to be done differently. What are your financial strengths? Your assets? Your previous debt? Your liquidity? Is the business financially sustainable in today's economy based upon the current numbers? Are the projections sound or are they based on a best-case financial scenario? Can the business survive a worst-case financial scenario? Do you have new opportunities for financing? Your Finance S.O.D. will begin to trigger ideas that can be used in your 1-PSP.

2. Select two objectives and define S.M.A.R.T. goals that can help you achieve your objectives.

3. List tactics or steps to take in achieving the broader goal.

4. Define what success looks like and list it as the result.

Finance S.O.D. (Strengths, Opportunities, Dangers)

Strengths	
Opportunities	
Dangers	

Finance Strategy

Objectives

Goals

Tactics

Results

12-Month Cash Flow

	Start-up	Month 1	Month 2	Month 3	Month 4	Month 5	Month 6	Month 7	Month 8	Month 9	Month 10	Month 11	Month 12	Year 1 Total
Beg. Cash Receipts														
Loan Equity														
TOTAL CASH														
COGS														
Officer's Salary														
Sub-Contract Labor														
Payroll Taxes														
Rent														
Utilities														
Telephone														
Maintenance														
Insurance														
Advertising														
Office Expense														
Supplies														
Professional Fees														
License														
Bank Charges														
Travel & Entertain														
Furniture & Fixture														
Equipment														
Misc. or 10% Contingency														
TOTAL EXPENSE														
NET CASH OUTLAY														
Loan														
End Cash														

Transform ~ Innovate ~ Stabilize ~ **Grow**

Marketing Strategy

Strategic Planning

Grow

Marketing Strategy

Research	7-TMP	Developing Your Message	Marketing Process
Research Your Marketplace	Complete the Seven-Touch Marketing Plan	Write your Benefits Message	Complete the Marketing Process identifying at least two goals
Understand Your Marketplace Your Industry Your Customers Your Competitors	Identify a Target Market Select seven methods of reaching the target market Calculate the cost of implementation	Define Product Benefits Determine how to reach your customers Write message to connect customers with benefits	Utilizing the S.T.A.R. analysis select two goals Define tactics and results for each Complete the Marketing Strategy section of 1-PSP
Research	7-TMP	Message	1-PSP Marketing Strategy

Marketing Strategy

Growing a business is not as easy as paying for advertising and waiting for your customers to open your door. It takes careful identification of WHO your customers are and HOW you are going to reach them.

A marketing S.T.A.R. begins with focusing on the strategic marketing plans to identify each target audience who can use your product or service then what methods of advertising will reach the buyer. The possibilities are endless so do not expect to be all things to everyone.

1. **Strategize** – Who is your target market? What are your goals for increasing sales and growing your business?

2. **Target** – Do you have the financial resources to achieve the objectives and goals identified? Are your goals S.M.A.R.T.?

3. **Act** – What specific steps are necessary to achieve the goals set above? How are you going to implement your marketing strategy?

4. **Reflect** – What worked and what did not work? Did you attract additional customers in the target market? Did you increase the number of returning customers? Did you increase sales? What needs to be done differently?

Focusing on a target market is not new, but the tools that we use to reach our customers (who may be on the other side of the globe) are new. You need to literally reach out and touch someone you cannot see or understand when they speak.

What is Marketing?

"Marketing is everything you do to promote your business, from the moment you conceive of it to the point at which customers buy your product or service and begin to patronize your business on a regular basis." – *Jay Conrad Levinson*

Emphasis should be placed on 'everything' and 'regular basis.' It is not just to put advertisements in a newspaper. Today this is more important than ever because it is so easy to throw up a blog and become too busy to manage it. Be careful what message you send.

Marketing includes concepts, promotional content, and promotional media in a wide gamut of topics: product, price, promotion, placement, service, manufacturing, or retail, market research, marketing strategy, advertising, marketing management, branding, direct marketing, personal sales, product placement, public relations, publicity, printing, sales promotion, underwriting, publication, broadcasting, out-of-home Internet marketing, point of sale, novelty items, digital marketing, in-game, and word of mouth.

Utilizing a multi-channel marketing approach that continually touches your target customers will reach them without becoming annoying.

How Can You Grow Your Business?

There are three basic ways to grow your business:

1. Increase the number of customers
2. Increase the number of times each customer buys
3. Increase the quantity that is sold each time

You can increase the number of customers using your existing product or service or you can increase the offering. You can expand your existing market or reach into new markets, but do your homework first. Which markets will be the most profitable?

Make it easy for your existing customers to do business with you. Be responsive to your customer's calls; be accessible when they contact you; be consistent with your offering; follow-up and follow through; and be accurate and timely with your billing.

Determine how you can add value and expand your service offering. If you stay customer focused, you will build a strong foundation for generating more sales, retaining more customers, and growing your business.

Marketing Misconceptions

There are several misconceptions about marketing that pose a threat to an effective marketing plan. Unrealistic expectations are a barrier to success and will prevent business owners from creating a plan that will succeed.

1. **One Strategy** – A common misconception that small business owners have is that if they use one marketing method they will eventually be successful. For example, they focus on newspaper advertising, excluding all other methods of reaching customers. They rationalize that they are saving money and that the consistency will pay off in the long run. Implementing only one of the marketing methods such as direct mail, brochures, phonebook advertisements, or telemarketing can prevent the business owner from reaching their target audience. It is a necessity not a luxury to diversifying marketing media.

2. **Clever vs. concise and clear** – Clever may be great in mystery stories and comedy shows but not in advertising. Do not make your customers guess what your product will do for them. Small business ads must be factual not entertaining. They must be easy to understand and focus on meeting the needs of the customer.

3. **Impatience** – Whatever the market method, it takes time to be effective and generate a profit. A business owner should not expect a miracle to happen overnight. It is important to have patience and give the campaign time to be successful.

Marketing plans are critical to the success of a business. The phrase 'build it and they will come' only happens in movies and on TV. The business must get the word out on different levels using various methods. Remember it takes seven touches to motivate your customer to buy your product. Imagine printing newspapers then leaving them stacked on the street corner rather than delivering them to the customer's door. Customers would miss the information unless they happened to walk by the stack and pick one up.

Regardless of the method, success comes from having a clear message and getting the word out to the potential customers.

Ten Ways to Grow Your Business

In an article written in May, 2004, Karen E. Spaeder correctly assesses the situation that many of you are in today. You spent considerable time and energy to get your business off the ground and now you are in a quandary on how to take your business to the next level.

For those of you who have survived startup and built successful businesses, you may be wondering how to take the next step and grow your business beyond its current status. Choosing the proper strategy now will make the difference between success and failure. What growth strategy you define in your strategic plan will depend on the type of business you own, your available resources, and how much money, time, and sweat equity you are willing to invest all over again.

The ten ways to grow your business are:

1. **Open another location**. Before you take the leap and open another location, consider the research that was required before you opened the current location(s). Choosing a new location requires careful research, planning, and number-crunching.

    -   Make sure you create a business plan for each new location.
    -   Make sure you know your management team and are prepared with a Plan B.
    -   Watch the bottom line!!
    -   Always choose a location that is best for the business not what is best for your wallet.

2. **Offer your business as a franchise or business opportunity**. Franchising is a model for expansion with an operating system that allows ownership on the part of the staff operating the franchise. The franchisee has a vested interest in the success of the business. Begin by networking within the franchise community and become a member of the International Franchise Association. Find a good franchise attorney as well as a mentor who has been through the franchise process.

3. **License your product.** Licensing minimizes your risk to produce and sell your brand or product. It is low cost when compared to starting your own company. Before you license your product, make sure you work with an intellectual property attorney to ensure you do not lose control of your product or service.

4. **Form an alliance**. Select alliances either organizations or companies that mutually benefit from the relationship. Similar to the hot dog and hot dog bun, some businesses dovetail and enable you to expand your business without increasing your risk. Some are as simple as adding a link to your Web site and receiving a commission on the number of clicks. The key is to make sure the alliances are relevant. You need to align yourself with businesses that already have clients.

5. **Diversify.** Diversifying is an excellent growth strategy because it allows you to have multiple streams of income that can often fill seasonal voids, such as snow plowing in the winter and landscaping in the summer. Speaking and writing complement each other and can increase sales and profit margins. Often business plans include ideas on diversification. Forms of diversification include new services, new products, and new target markets.

6. **Target other markets.** Expand into uncharted territory and open new markets. Go global and retrofit your product so you can approach a new market. Brainstorm ideas on how your product or service can be used by a new group of customers.

7. **Win a government contract.** The U.S. government is the largest buyer of goods and services in the world, with total procurement dollars reaching approximately $235 billion in 2002. Work with the ISBDC or PTAC. Patience is a requirement when working with the government. Requests for proposals usually require a significant amount of groundwork and research. If you are not prepared to take the time to fully comply with RFP terms and conditions, you will only be wasting your time. The end result is worth it if you win a bid, because you generally do not have to go through the same legwork next time.

8. **Merge with or acquire another business.** While on the surface this appears to be a great opportunity and it can be very successful, there are a number of issues that must be addressed: customer retention, staff retention, technologies integration, and defining the merged culture.

9. **Expand globally.** You can go global with any of the solutions already mentioned. To build an international strategy, you need to consider the need for a foreign distributor who will carry an inventory of your product and resell it in their domestic markets. You can locate foreign distributors by scouring your city or state for a foreign company with a U.S. representative. Other good places to find distributors who you can work with include trade groups, foreign Chambers of Commerce in the United States, and branches of American Chambers of Commerce in foreign countries.

10. **Expand to the Internet.** "Bill Gates said that by the end of 2002, there will be only two kinds of businesses: Those with an Internet presence, and those with no business at all," notes Sally Falkowa, Pasadena, California, Web content strategist. "Perhaps this is overstating the case, but an effective Web site is becoming an integral part of business today." The focus is on Search Engine Optimization and keeping your customer on your site so they will buy your product or service.

You need a Web site that is ranked high enough to ensure adequate traffic and designed well enough that it looks professional. It is also very important that there is content that is relevant so it draws in visitors and they stay.

In the space provided below, list ways to grow your business. Be creative and think outside the box.

1.	
2.	
3.	
4.	
5.	
6.	
7.	
8.	

A key point to always remember is 'Never stop growing the business!' You cannot afford to take a month off from marketing your business.

Understanding Your Marketplace

The Industry

Retail: Defined by the products you sell.
Service: Defined by services you provide.
Manufacturing: Defined by the products you manufacture.

It is very important to know what industry you are in so you can define who your competitors are and analyze the opportunity and danger they pose to your business. Start by identifying the NAICS and SIC that correspond to your business.

Search www.census.gov/epcd/www/naics.html to determine the appropriate Standard Industrial Classification Manual (SIC) and North American Industry Classification System (NAICS).

NAICS 611430 Professional and Management Development Training

This industry comprises establishments primarily engaged in offering an array of short-duration courses and seminars for management and professional development. Training for career development may be provided directly to individuals or through employers' training programs; and courses may be customized or modified to meet the special needs of customers. Instruction may be provided in diverse settings, such as the establishment's or client's training facilities, educational institutions, the workplace, or the home, and through correspondence, television, Internet, or other means.

SCHOOLS AND EDUCATIONAL SERVICES (SIC 8299)

Establishments primarily engaged in offering specialized educational courses and services, not elsewhere classified, such as music schools, drama schools, language schools, student exchange programs, and civil service and other short-term examination preparatory schools. Vocational counseling (excluding rehabilitation) is also included here. Educational testing is included in Industry 8748. Establishments primarily engaged in operating dance schools are classified in Industry 7911; those providing rehabilitation counseling are classified in Industry 8331; and those providing sports instruction in Industry 7999.

As you research the industry, there are additional resources available from professional associations. What trade association to join? What publications to subscribe to? What trade shows to attend?

More Industry Research

Complete the information below by searching the Internet or exploring a library.

Business Description: _____

Industry: _____

SIC Code: _____ NAICS Code: _____

National Trade Association   / Address, e-Mail, phone number:

Regional or Local Trade Association / Address, e-Mail, phone number:

Trade Publications:

1. _____

2. _____

3. _____

Is the Industry:
- Beginning
- Growing
- Maturing
- Declining

What are the HOT products in this industry?

What are the HOT markets in this industry?

What are the declining products and markets?

Customers

How you market your product or service is a key to your business success.

Contrary to popular belief, Steve Jobs did not invent the Apple computer; he was responsible for marketing it. Steve Wozniak invented the first Apple computer. How well you market your business, along with a few other considerations, will determine your degree of success or failure. The key element of a successful marketing plan is to know your customers. Identifying who they are and what they like, dislike, and expect can help you develop a marketing strategy that allows you to meet their needs.

Narrow the Funnel

- Define your target customers.

   Note: Only 20% of your customers buy 80% of your product.
- Define the market:
   a) Geographically
   b) Demographically
   c) Related businesses (When you buy hot dogs, you also buy hot dog buns.)
   d) Lifestyle – Interests
   e) Terms of purchase – buy in bulk, first-time buyers

- Primary customers (indicate % of your business):
   a) Private sector   _____
   b) Wholesalers   _____
   c) Retailers   _____
   d) Government   _____
   e) Other   _____

- How much did the selected market spend on your type of product or service last year? $_____

Customer Detail

Define the characteristics of your ideal customers in as much detail as possible.

Age (Range)	
Sex (Male / Female)	
Income (Range)	
Occupation	
Education Level	
Home Address	
Lifestyle	
Geographical Location	
Other Business Variables	
Description of Business (if you sell to other businesses)	

Other details:

Competitors

Know your competitors. In the training field, online training started slower than most trainers expected, so it was discounted. It has, however, become a viable competitor to on-site training. Be honest and seek everyone who could take away even one customer.

1. Who are your three nearest direct competitors?

Name Address	Years in Business	Product/Service Feature	Market Share	Price Strategy

2. Who are your indirect competitors?

3. Are the competitors:
   Steady? Increasing? Decreasing?

4. What have you learned from their operations?

5. What can you learn from their advertising?

6. What are their strengths and weaknesses?

7. How does their product or service differ from yours?

How competitive is the market?

High	_____
Medium	_____
Low	_____

List your strengths and weaknesses compared to your competition. (Consider such areas as location, size of resources, reputation, services, personnel, etc.):

	Your Strengths		Your Weaknesses
1.		1.	
2.		2.	
3.		3.	
4.		4.	

Competitor Review

Define the characteristics of your competitors and how to get more information about them. If I am going to provide a new business training seminar, then my competitors might be classes provided by a business development center, the community colleges and high schools, online seminars, national conferences, and books.

List specific competitors below with ideas on how you can mitigate their competitive advantage. Addressing your competition is very important as you prepare your marketing plan.

Competitors	Action Plan

Pricing and Sale

Your pricing strategy is an important marketing technique if you choose to compete in the low-cost space. You need to balance the three price triggers: cost, quality, and customization. Get a feel for the pricing strategies your competitors are using. You need to balance these three triggers and market your products and services based on competitors in your market.

Some of the pricing strategies are:

- Retail cost plus your profit percentage
- Competitive position
- Pricing below competition
- Pricing above competition
- Price lining
- Multiple pricing
- Service costs plus your profit percentage
- Service components
- Material costs
- Labor costs
- Overhead costs

The key to success is to have a well-planned strategy! You need to understand your customers' expectations and how you plan to fulfill their needs. Monitor your price and your costs to ensure you are making a profit and periodically reevaluate where you are compared to your competitors and the entire industry's trends. The idea is to make a profit!

Advertising

How you advertise and promote your goods and services may make or break your business. If you have a great product, but you do not tell anyone, you will not be a business survivor. Forget the motto, "If I build it, they will come." No one will come if they are not invited. Great companies are great because they tell you they are great. Advertising and promotions are the lifeline of a business and should be treated as such.

Advertise and network to promote your business. You have options for shouting the advantages of your products so customers will buy them (including billboards and TV ads) but you can also pay $5 for a ream of paper to print 500 flyers! Build a plan and work the plan no matter who pressures you to stray. Make sure the advertisements you create are consistent with your business' image.

Promotional Plan

Image - What image do you want for your organization?

Is your image *Low-cost, Customization, High-quality, Fast, Innovative, or Customer-focused?*

What is your Elevator Speech? This is your thirty second commercial! Practice it, know it, and be ready in any elevator. Start by writing your Elevator Speech below.

Pricing

1. What is your pricing strategy? (Check which you use.)

   Markup on cost   _____   % markup   _____

   Suggested price   _____

   Competitive   _____

   Below competition   _____

   Premium price   _____

   Other   _____

2. Are your prices in line with your image?
   Yes____ No____

3. Do your prices cover costs and leave a margin of profit?
   Yes____ No____

Pricing Worksheet

List all of your products and services. For each one, determine what percent of your revenue will be from that product or service. You can make sub-categories if it makes it easier to determine the unit price and the number of units that must be sold to achieve your goals.

Products or Services	%	Retail Price	# of Units	Total $
Workshops	50%	$200	5	$1000
Game Sales	25%	$ 25	20	$ 500
Book Sales	25%	$ 25	20	$ 500
Total	100%			$2000

The retail price is based on the actual costs of the product or service plus a markup determined by the market and your pricing strategy. Do not set a unit price less than your costs including your time. You cannot succeed in business if you do.

Products or Services	%	Retail Price	# of Units	Total $
Total				

Customer Services

List the customer services you provide.

1. _____
2. _____
3. _____

Advertising

Which advertising or promotion sources do you intend to use?

Television	_____
Radio	_____
Direct mail	_____
Personal contacts	_____
Trade Associations	_____
Newspaper	_____
Magazines	_____
Yellow Pages	_____
Billboard	_____
Other	_____

Why do you think the media you have chosen is the most effective?

Developing Your Message

A marketing plan is vital to the survival and success of a small business. When resources are limited, it becomes even more important that the plan identify how to reach the customers who will buy the specific product or service. When competing for customers, the business that makes the fewest mistakes will be the survivor.

Planning to fail is the result of marketing without a plan.

It takes more than one time to reach a customer. Research indicates that it requires seven touches with a consistent message to make a sale.

Step One: Know who your customers are.

Who do you sell to? Who do you want to sell to? In the space below, use the information you collected about your marketplace to describe one of your customers.

| |
| |

Where do your customers go to get information about your product or service?

| 1. |
| 2. |
| 3. |
| 4. |

Step Two: Know the benefits of your product or service from your customer's perspective.

Look at your product or service and define the benefits to your customers. Features are nice, but they do not make the sale. Your customer must be convinced that the benefit is worth the cost to purchase the product or service. The benefit for each customer will be different. If you sell to both consumers and other businesses, create two lists of benefits and create two separate marketing plans.

An example of a feature is the time and place a training session is offered. The benefit to the customer is the convenience of the timing and dates when the class is held. Features are specific descriptions of the product or service, i.e., the color is red. A benefit is why it is good for the customer, i.e., the new color trend will brighten your day.

Product or Service	Customer	Benefit

From your list of benefits, create a message that will resonate with one of your customers. As you market your product, it is important that the message stay consistent.

Step Three: Connect your customer with the message.

This step is all about the tools. At PartyPro.com they use the Internet and a robust Web site to reach their customers. How do you reach your customers?

1.
2.
3.
4.

Putting an ad in a newspaper once is not an example of an effective marketing strategy. Review the list of major media types to identify new methods that you can use to reach your customers seven times.

Describe below one method that you can use to touch your customers. How is this different from plans to reach other target markets? How will you separate the messages to ensure that the customers only hear the message that is targeting them?

How much will it cost to implement the marketing method?
$ _____

How many times will you need to utilize the method to consistently reach your customer base? _____

What are the risks? _____

When do you expect results? _____

Are your goals S.M.A.R.T.? _____

Major Media Types (www.iesmallbusiness.com/resources)

Media	Advantages	Limitations	Cost
Newspapers	Flexibility; timeliness; good local market coverage; broad acceptability; high believability; expanding online	Short life; poor reproduction quality; small pass-along audience; declining audience	$1,300 / week for 2" x 2" ad This depends on the newspaper!
Television	Good mass market coverage; low cost per exposure; combines sight, sound, & motion; appealing to the senses	High absolute costs; high clutter; fleeting exposure; less audience selectivity	$200,000 for one 30-second commercial (during prime-time)
Direct Mail	High audience selectivity; flexibility; no ad competition within the same medium; allows personalization	Relatively high cost per exposure; 'junk mail' image	$1,500 for 1,000 4x6 postcards (includes postage)
Radio	Good local acceptance; high geographic and demographic selectivity; low cost	Audio only, fleeting exposure; low attention (the 'half-heard' medium); fragmented audiences	$90 to $120 per week on a rotator (prices higher if time slots for ad are selective)
Magazines	High and demographic selectivity; credibility and prestige; high-quality reproduction; long life and good pass-along readership	Long ad purchase lead-time; high cost; no guarantee of position	$1,200 to $5,000 per month or per issue (depends on ad size and demographics)
Outdoor (Billboard)	Flexibility; high repeat exposure; low cost; low message competition; good positional selectivity	Little audience selectivity, creative limitations	$3,000 artwork; $5,000 to $500,000; Minimum contract is 16 weeks
Online	High selectivity; low cost; immediacy; interactive capabilities; increased coverage; new options for precise delivery	Small, demographi-cally skewed audience; audience controls exposure	$0.60 pay-per-click, $1,800 / month aggressive campaigns; $200- to- $1,200 per year per banner ad

Web Site – A Tool

A Web site is a tool to reach more customers but like any tool, i.e., hammer, shovel, rolling pin, etc., the tool is not effective without a human hand to guide it. You have to direct the use of your Web site. You need to advertise using other methods to drive customers to the Web site. A Web site is the perfect place to state the message. Elaborate on the benefits to the customers. It is easy to create multiple messages for multiple customers (target markets).

How can you use a Web site to grow your business? What methods can you use to ensure your customers read your message?

1.
2.
3.
4.

What are your S.M.A.R.T. goals for your Web site?

Other Marketing Opportunities

When considering all the potential marketing ideas and looking for more diversity in our Seven-Touch Marketing Plan (7-TMP), we should not overlook "low-cost" opportunities. Below are just a few, but they may spur your own creativity   so do not be afraid to try something different.

Blogs – If you are utilizing a Web site to market your business, consider adding a Blog. This does not have to be elaborate or time-consuming. In fact, the shorter, the better. The important thing to remember is to provide information, tell a pertinent story or address a common concern. This will drive attention to your site and also establishes you as a subject matter expert. By implementing a Blog you can become the 'go-to' person in the industry!

News Articles – Many times we consider newspapers as only a resource for displaying ads. Perhaps you were not aware that many local, and even some larger news media, encourage local writers to submit newsworthy articles. The papers review these articles, edit them and then use them to fill 'white' space in the paper. Consider writing articles about your business, your industry, and solutions you can provide. Add a photo and your chances go up that the article will be printed, not to mention the attention it will bring you!

Press Releases and Media Events – Maybe you created a press release when you launched your business. Did you know, you can submit press releases any time you want to announce something going on at your business? So why not get creative? Invite a local celebrity to a special event at your business and get the media involved. The local celebrity could be a civic leader, a teacher, a local young athlete or a Boy Scout Troop.

Partner With a Charity – Communities always love to see a business involved with the neighborhood. What better way to say, "We are here to serve" than by opening your business up to host a local charity event.

You provide the location, the charity does the rest! Or maybe you can help fund some of the promotional costs by paying for flyers, providing materials (water for a car wash) or offering the workers light refreshments.

Event Days – Instead of advertising a sale or special promotion, couple the event with a token of appreciation to your customers. Offer free soft drinks, coffee, donuts, pretzels, hot dogs, candy treats or whatever you can imagine. Something small in exchange for coming by is sure to help spur reciprocity!

Marketing is key to growing your business. When economic times are tough, marketing becomes essential to survival. However, it does not have to break the bank. Get creative and innovate new ideas that minimize your marketing expenses!

Seven-Touch Marketing Plan (7-TMP)

1. Determine your target market(s).
2. Select seven methods to 'touch' your current and potential customers.
3. Decide on the frequency that you are going to use these methods.
4. Calculate the cost for each method and the total cost.
5. Adjust the method and frequency until the total cost equals what you have in your budget.

	Target Market	Seven-Touch Methods	Frequency	Cost
1.				
2.				
3.				
4.				
5.				
6.				
7.				
			Total Cost	

Marketing Strategic Planning

Consistency in expressing your message using a variety of methods is important as you develop a Marketing Strategy.

1. Start with a Marketing S.O.D. Look at your current Marketing Plan and decide what needs to be done differently. What are the messages that are important to your success? What are your strengths? What opportunities do you have to improve your market share? What new approaches will make a difference? What are the dangers if you do not try innovative new solutions? Your Marketing S.O.D. will begin to trigger ideas that can be used in your 1-PSP.

2. Select two objectives and define S.M.A.R.T. goals that can help you achieve your objectives.

3. List tactics or steps to take in achieving the broader goal.

4. Define what success looks like and list it as the result.

Marketing S.O.D. (Strengths, Opportunities, Dangers)

Strengths	
Opportunities	
Dangers	

Marketing Strategy

Objectives

Goals

Tactics

Results

Seven-Touch Marketing Plan (7-TMP)

This report indicates the customers, the methods used to penetrate the market, and the estimated budget necessary to implement the marketing strategy.

	Target Market	Seven-Touch Methods	Frequency	Cost
1.				
2.				
3.				
4.				
5.				
6.				
7.				
			Total Cost	

Transform ~ Innovate ~ Stabilize ~ Grow

Action

Strategic Planning			
Action			
Implementation			
Action Planning	**S.T.A.R. Process**	**Review the Plan**	**Life Plan**
Create an Action Plan	Review S.T.A.R. Planning Process	Use Checklist to review	Prepare for Life
Review STAR Material With the 1-PSP, 1-PRC, 12-MCF, 7-TMP prepare a 1-PAP Define priorities and critical path	Review Strategic Plan Define targets Implement the Plan Reflect and review the plan	Use four checklists to ensure you have completed all of the required tasks Make changes as needed	Define your long range goals Ensure that your life is in balance
1-PAP	Action Plans	Checklists	Life Balance

Implementation

Your **1-PSP** is a living document that should change and evolve over time. Where are you on the timeline continuum? Are you still in the initial stage of exploring ideas? Do you have a business plan that you think will work for you? Have you developed plans to accomplish the milestones in your **1-PSP**? Are you making the progress you expected? Do you want to change your direction? Identify what you have accomplished and what you need to work on. Decide what is on first and list it below. You are in the driver's seat, so make it happen.

What have you accomplished?

What do you need to work on?

Identify what needs to be done first, second, and third. It is easy to take smaller steps as you start your tasks. Indicate the priority in completing each item listed above.

Action Planning

To make your One-Page Strategic Plan happen, you will need to use planning skills in the same way you would plan an event. It is not any different than planning a birthday party or a team-building session. You define what you want to accomplish then divide it into smaller tasks that are assigned to people to complete. You set a budget and deadlines when the tasks need to be done.

Creating a 1-PAP (One-Page Action Plan) does not have to be complex or labor intensive. You do not need expensive software to track the initiative, but you do need to plan. You need to answer a few simple questions. What needs to be done? When does it need to be done? How much will it cost? Who needs to do it?

The four stages of action planning are:

1. **Strategize** – Initial planning summarized on a 1-PSP.

2. **Target** – Goals broken down into multiple tactics that are assigned to an individual and given a budget, then tracked with a 1-PAP until completed.

3. **Act** – Implement your plan. Just do it! And while you are doing it, monitor your progress, identify the status and record your results.

4. **Reflect** – Ask simple questions to determine what went well and what should be done differently in the future.

Stage 1 – Strategize

The Strategize phase of the S.T.A.R. process starts with the completion of your 1-PSP (One-Page Strategic Plan).

The 1-PSP identifies the strategic area and objective. It is the scope of the plan with specific goals that relate to the overall vision. It lists the tactics to achieve the goals and measurements to know when the goals are completed.

This stage is where you think out-of-the-box to reach new conclusions and reinvent your business to strengthen it and survive. The 1-PSP is the outcome of this stage.

The thought process should include identification of problems and determining the feasibility of the solutions you identify. The 1-PSP helps all of the stakeholders understand the priorities and become committed to achieving the objectives outlined in the 1-PSP. The document helps focus the activity and provides balance in making assignments that ensure a balanced success. One strategic area is not neglected because it is not a crisis. Scope creep and activity traps are avoided when the objectives are clear and balanced.

When creating a 1-PSP, challenge assumptions, investigate new approaches, and explore out-of-the-box solutions. Invent new methods and be willing to step out of your comfort zone. In challenging economic and environmental times, new ideas become the future model of success.

Your objective is to be a S.T.A.R and reinvent your business to transform it into a highly-successful organization.

Review of the 1-PSP Goals and Objectives

Before focusing on the details of your strategic plan, it is important to establish objectives and straightforward goals for each strategic area then focus on the tactics. These define the plan and influence how we measure success. To be sure that the goals and objectives are clearly written and appropriate, it is important to subject the goals to the 'S.M.A.R.T.' test.

S — Specific: Is it specific in completing the goal or tactic?

M — Measurable: What are the indicators of progress or success?

A — Attainable: Can it be achieved within the resources and time allowed?

R — Relevant: Is it important for the direction you are taking the business?

T — Time-bound: Is there a timeframe when the goal will be completed?

Measure of Success

The goals should be measured to help determine success. You must choose some measurable criteria. It might be the number of customers, a change in the frequency of a given activity, or a change in behavior. Remember that it is difficult to measure intangibles like attitude or knowledge without some formal assessment or test. Goals that use qualifying words like 'all' or 'never' are also difficult to achieve. However, terms like 'increase' and 'decrease' paired with quantitative percentages, ratios, volumes, dollars or similar words make for very clear expectations. The desired results are recorded along with the steps to achieve the goals.

Tactic, Approach, or Method

How will you tackle the plan? It is important to consider the assumptions and risks to success before making this decision. Often the approach or method chosen is a direct result of what you think is the best way to overcome those roadblocks to success. In addition, you need to consider if the way you have always done this type of plan is the most effective. You may sometimes work on a task that has never been done before and that causes you to consider several approaches or methods. Use this opportunity to think out-of-the-box to come up with novel approaches to achieving the objectives.

Be innovative! In general, when we work on something we have done before, we tend to use the same methods that have been used in the past. But we have all heard the old saying: "If you do what you have always done, you will get what you have always gotten." Think about it, is 'what we have always gotten' what we always wanted? If the same marketing method achieves poor results, why would you want to keep utilizing the same methods?

The selection of the best possible approach or method may well constitute the most important decision you make during the early stages of planning. That selection influences everything that follows. Therefore, special consideration should always be given when you create the 1-PSP.

Here are some guidelines to help you choose a tactic, approach, or method:

- Focus on high-level objectives then on the goals to achieve them.
- Challenge assumptions regarding previous tactics, approaches, and methods.
- Explore out-of-the-box solutions.
- Do not hesitate to invent new methods and tactics.

Even if you are working on stabilizing your finances and operations, you should be innovative as you transform your business.

Assumptions or Risks

We use a S.O.D. to define assumptions and risks. What are your strengths, opportunities, and dangers? When they are written down they can lay a clear path to success. A S.O.D. clarifies the direction you should take. Objectives, goals, and tactics help you understand the plan's implications and assists with planning your strategies.

Assumptions (strengths, opportunities, and dangers) are attitudes that are widely held concerning the plan. Some of them may be factual while others may not be factual; however, they determine your plan of action. Risks or dangers are those things that could undermine the success of the plan.

To help you identify assumptions or risks, answer the following questions for each objective:

- What resources are required to realistically complete the goals and tactics identified in this 1-PSP?
- What dangers are associated with obtaining the resources in a timely manner?
- What problems or delays are likely to occur in completing each objective?
- What effect will delays have on the overall action plan and schedule?

With an honest S.O.D. completed, take another look at the 1-PSP.

Will it push the plan forward or should another approach be adopted? Remember that the approach is often the key to a successful plan. Be sure that the chosen approach is the right one for the plan in light of the objectives, assumptions, and risks. Before you throw out any approaches in favor of a single one, consider each one as a potential 'back-up' approach. In this way, you can prioritize approaches and be able to change direction should unforeseen events occur.

Creating a 1-PSP avoids the trap of jumping in without a plan and making mistakes. Without a plan you will waste time and resources as you decide what to do next. The second trap is called 'scope creep.' That is where the original scope of the 1-PSP is not clearly defined and someone says, 'Oh, while you are at it, do this, too.' Such 'add-ons' can escalate the investment of time and other resources. A clearly-defined plan helps you determine when add-ons are not a part of the plan and can be done later.

Stage 2 – Target

In Stage Two of the strategic planning process, you will move information from a One-Page Strategic Plan (1-PSP) to a One-Page Action Plan (1-PAP) where the tactics (approaches and methods) are listed under their associated goal and assigned to an individual or individuals along with a budget and completion date. This is the detail planning stage where the ideas are brought from a high level strategic focus to a practical 'How are we going to get it done?' level.

If the strategic plan is not complex, then a 1-PAP can be used to identify basic information about the tactics assigned to each goal. Additionally, project management software, if available, can be used to build the implementation plan.

The 1-PAP is used to identify, define, and distribute the workload of the plan. It divides each goal into the separate tactics that are necessary to accomplish the goal and puts the activities in order so you see what must be done, when, and by whom. It also identifies activities that can be completed simultaneously or may require a logical sequence to be followed.

Finally, it helps to identify when and where some activities are being needlessly duplicated. By identifying them in the **1-PAP** before actually performing them, we save on valuable resources (time, money, and manpower).

The tactics, like the goals, should pass the S.M.A.R.T. test. Tactics should follow specific guidelines:
- Each tactic should have a definite start and stop time.
- They should have an expected result.
- They may be linked to one another, but they should not overlap.
- The time and cost of each tactic should be easy to define.
- Every tactic should be assignable to an individual and easily accomplished by them. (If not, the activity should probably be divided further.)

One idea to assist in creating the **1-PAP** is to record each tactic on a sticky note with one tactic per sticky note so they can be moved around and placed in the correct order. If more than one person will be working on the tactics, you can use different color sticky notes to represent each person. Once the tactics have all been identified, the order clearly defined, and the responsible individual for each tactic assigned, the tactics can be put in Excel, Word, or Project Management software.

Giving careful thought to the order of tactics can be critical to the success of the strategic plan. Putting all the tactics in random order often makes the plan too long to complete and is not efficient in accomplishing the objectives. While some things cannot be started until another part of the plan has been completed, often several tactics can be accomplished simultaneously. Ordering the tactics helps facilitate linking and establishing a critical path. A critical path is the alignment of required tactics. When required tactics are placed in an order so the plan will be completed in the shortest timeframe, efficiency is generally the outcome.

If you use sticky notes on flipchart paper, you can use a marker to draw lines between tactics that are linked to one another. If different color sticky notes are used for different individuals, you will see at a glance dependencies and overload.

Plans usually have one or more sets of linked activities. The longest one of these is sometimes called the critical path — that is, the set of required linked tactics that you will need to watch closely. A tactic, along the critical path that is not completed when scheduled, will most likely lead to a delay with the overall plan.

To be innovative in transforming your business, you need to:
- Challenge assumptions.
- Think 'out-of-the-box.
- Be pioneering.
- Do not be trapped in doing what has always been done.

Once the 1-PAP is documented and ready to be shared with others, there are important guidelines to follow.
- Everyone must clearly understand the purpose of the overall plan.
- Each individual must understand his or her assignment – their purpose.
- Each individual needs to know the details of each assigned tactic, the availability of resources, and the plan's duration.
- Individual's skills and resources must be matched to tactics.
- Reporting times must be established so everyone is informed on the plan's progress.
- The team members must understand their responsibility in providing status in a timely manner.
- Define milestones and celebrations along the way, so progress is visible to everyone and forward momentum is maintained.

The sample 1-PAP shows the relationship between the 1-PSP and the action plan required to implement it. Each strategy has a page in the action plan. The objectives and goals are defined in more detail but they relate directly to the strategy. Results on the 1-PSP are defined on the 1-PAP adding clarity and focus.

Progress is monitored on the 1-PAP with colorful indicators to show progress in accomplishing the goals.

I-PSP

1-PSP (One-Page Strategic Plan)

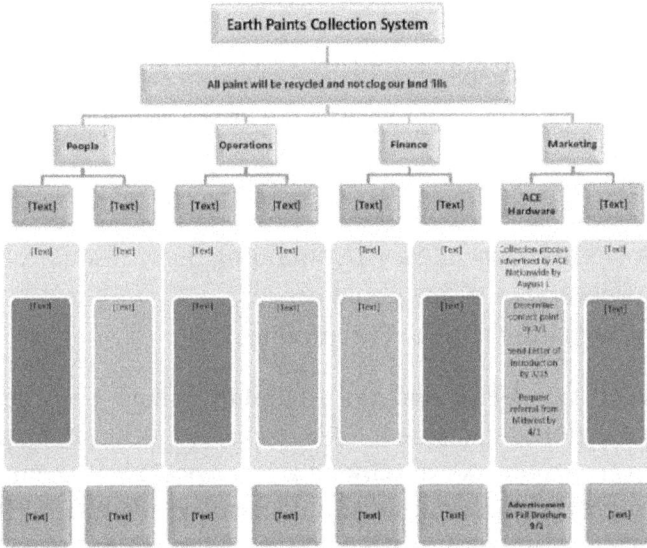

1-PAP (Roadmap)

1-PAP (One-Page Action Plan)

Strategy	**Marketing**						
Objective	**Ace Hardware**			Completion Date	**September 1**		

Goal	Tactic	Completion Date	Responsibility	Cost	Result	Achieved (Yes / No)	
Collection process advertised by ACE Nationwide by August 1	1. Determine contact point by 3/1	3/1	George	$0	Name to Contact	Yes	◐
	2. Send Letter of introduction by 3/15	3/15	George	$0	Letter sent	Yes	◐
	3. Request referral from Midwest by 4/1	4/1	George	$0	Midwest Manager communication		○
	4. Support ACE Promotion Campaign by 9/1	9/1	George	$0	Advertisement in Fall Brochure 9/1		●
	5.						
	6.						

Project management software tracks projects in more detail and can indicate overloads and conflicts between allocated resources. Critical paths and other charts are easily printed to show priorities in completing the assigned tasks across the business. Timelines and milestones are tracked and monitored to ensure an on-time delivery.

At this stage it is important to assess risk and plan how to avoid delays. Ask questions such as:

- What resources are required?
- What risks are associated with obtaining these resources?
- What problems or delays could occur?
- What effects might any delays produce?

The tactics on the 1-PSP and the roadmap should be ordered by what must be done and when. The document is used to provide clarity so everyone knows exactly what is expected of them. Timelines and reporting procedures should also be identified. It is all about knowing exactly what needs to be done when, how, where, and by whom.

Every tactic and goal must pass the S.M.A.R.T. test. For example, there must be clear start and stop dates, defined time and cost estimates, responsible individuals assigned and authority given. If you are the sole person working on the tactics, be realistic on what can be done in a specified timeframe. Expect the unexpected and include time to do the normal day-to-day tasks. Be careful to avoid burn-out by overloading yourself or someone else. Realistic is the keyword when developing the 1-PAP.

Stage 3 – Act

Stage Three is where you put the plan in action and the vision becomes reality. You must stay motivated to get the job done yourself and to be able to motivate others. It is leadership and focus. It is determination to get the job done and get it done right. Implementing may include utilizing additional resources.

At this point there will be decision making and problem solving. As you implement the 1-PAP, you will make changes and modifications depending on circumstances and changes in your business to achieve the desired results.

Putting the plan in action and doing it! It is all about implementing the plan. Creating a strategic plan (1-PSP) then the roadmap (1-PAP) and storing it on a shelf or in a drawer will not move your business forward. Now is the time to do it. The roadmap is available, so follow it!

Whether you are a small business owner with or without employees, you are responsible for motivating those around you who will help you accomplish the tasks. If you already have a strong team with a banker, accountant, attorney, insurance agent, etc., meet with them and let them know how your strategic plan will involve or impact them. Get their advice and share your vision. If you do not have a strong team assisting you, then consider forming one as a possible objective for your 1-PSP.

Your leadership style will change depending on what is needed and how experienced the individuals are. Sometimes they will only need information about resources from you; and at other times, they will need specific directions or clarity on the direction you are planning to take. They may need support and encouragement or assistance in solving a problem.

To meet timelines and stay on track, always stay mindful of the critical path and set priorities so deadlines are met on or before they are expected. At times additional resources may be needed to ensure that the tactics are completed on time. Stay alert and on the lookout for these possibilities.

Make sure that you do not micromanage the assignments made to others. Give them the freedom to work in their own way as long as the timeline is on target to finish as expected. Trust is vital to a small business's success. At the same time remember you cannot expect what you do not inspect. So trust but verify.

SMALL BUSINESS STRATEGIC PLANNING

Progress needs to be monitored to determine changes in priority and resources. Unexpected circumstances may require you to restart the process or focus on another strategic area. The key is to be aware of changes around you and stick to the plan as long as it is feasible. When you determine that the situation calls for a change in direction do not hesitate. Be decisive. Pull out the appropriate backup plan and move forward.

Reporting During the Action Phase

Using color indications on the 1-PAP can help you monitor and track your progress. The 1-PAP provides a common tool for reporting progress and sets clear expectations on how to report the status of each tactic.

As with any plan, communication is vital to success by helping all parties work together. The report is a visual methodology to clearly see when tasks are not done that might affect the entire strategic plan. Some deadlines are more flexible than others. To color code the chart provides further clarity and a higher impact on the team.

Reporting tools are available that provide detail charts that track progress as does Excel. These tools are an excellent way to show progress in more detail than the 1-PAP but they are not necessary and require an expertise in using the software.

The bottom line is you need to focus on the objectives and clearly have the end in mind. Your commitment to your business is reflected in your determination to achieve the desired results. You will transform your business as you work on your 1-PAP.

Roadmap

Your 1-PAP is your roadmap to reaching your goals through strategic measurements. It is your action plan and is also called the roadmap because it views the lifecycle of the goals. In other words, from the highest level of creation, the strategy through the implementation stage using tactics produces a roadmap displaying where and how well progress is being made during the process.

A dashboard signal may be provided on the roadmap to visually represent a specific goal's status toward achieving the results indicated on the chart. Sometimes this signal indicates the status of a specific goal or the goal of a key performance indicator. The Key Performance Indicator (KPI) is a goal selected by the management team as one which is critical to the success of the strategic plan.

KPI (Key Performance Indicators) characteristics include:

- Percent Completed
- Funds Spent / Funds Allocated
- Time to Completion
- Percent On-Target
- Percent Started

What you measure, you may achieve at the expense of other indicators. If you rush to meet an unrealistic deadline, the quality of the results may not be what you expect. If you spend an hour painting a room rather than the day you allocated, the paint may be applied unevenly and the cleanup may take longer than expected. But the project was completed on time and within budget.

Targets and key indicators must be carefully selected based on strategic goals so you measure what you want to achieve. Think through the implications of selecting specific measurements. Analyze the unplanned consequences of selecting the measurements and document what you do not want to happen.

There are hundreds of measurements that you can use to monitor progress; select only a couple. In this case fewer is better. The other indicators can be used occasionally but stick with the ones that can be tied to your strategies.

S.M.A.R.T. goals are the basic building blocks to keep a business focused on the activities and efforts necessary for sustainable success. They remove barriers of confusion and indecisiveness. Once understood and practiced, they become a fundamental part of everyday business.

Managing all of the tracking data on one page is vital to success. The easier it is to track the completion of tactics and goals, the greater the chances for success. Like any good habit, success breeds continued use and success.

Stage 4 – Reflect

The final stage before you start again is to celebrate the accomplishments and then to reflect on the process and outcomes to determine changes that need to be made.

When the action plan is complete, there are still two important things to do. One is to recognize your accomplishments. The second is to complete an action plan review. This evaluation should be written and include an analysis of several things including:

- Were the goals and objectives met?
- Was the plan completed on time?
- How might we make things run better next time?

This written report will enable you to remember what happened and how to avoid some of the pitfalls you may have encountered. The purpose of this review is to evaluate what happened and why. This is important because we want to identify what can be done in future activities to improve the results achieved in this action plan.

During this review process, there are several things to keep in mind. For example, if you are working with a team of employees, it is important that the review process remain positive and blame-free. The environment must remain open and promote candor from all participants. Identify and link the lessons learned to solutions to be implemented on future action plans.

As a small business owner, this review process provides an insight into how you are running your business and how your organization is working. It supports the use of common metrics and measurements that can be used to track initiatives across the business. Most of all it helps you develop a clearer vision of the improvements you make to sustain and grow your business. It is the formula for strategic planning and success!

Let us review the four stages of action planning: 1) strategize, 2) target, 3) action, and 4) reflect. This four-stage method of strategic planning will enable you to achieve greater success. Key elements are the 1-PSP and 1-PAP. The action plan review is a time to reflect on what was learned and serves as a basis for the next plan.

Your Challenge

Today, find a trusted advisor who you can report where you are in the business planning process; then check-in monthly, telling the advisor where you are on the journey. They are your lifeline to strategic planning, your accountability partner!

Remember to pay attention to what matters most and transform, innovate, stabilize, and grow your business to achieve sustainable success using the simple planning cycle of S.T.A.R. (Strategize, Target, Act, and Reflect).

Work your plan because only you can pull your vision together!

1-PAP (One-Page Action Plan)

Strategy

Objective

Goal	Tactic	Completion Date	Responsibility	Cost	Results	Achieved Yes / No

Completion Date: ⬤◯⬤

Reviewing Your Plan

We have examined ways to transform, innovate, stabilize, and grow your small businesses by addressing specific areas of the business including people, operations, finance, and marketing. For each of these areas individually, we have considered strategic options and focused on a methodology called S.T.A.R. to align objectives and goals. We have introduced tools and techniques, perhaps some are new and others, although known to us, have been shelved for various reasons. We have seen how a one-page strategic plan called the 1-PSP can help us identify what is important to our business. We know that a one-page action plan called the 1-PAP is our roadmap to success because it details how to implement our strategies and make them a reality.

To review, strategic planning includes the following outcomes designed to ensure sustainable growth.

- **One-Page Strategic Plan (1-PSP)**

  A strategic plan designed for a small business to survive and take their business to the next level.

- **One-Page Relationship Chart (1-PRC)**

  A list of key individuals who are essential to the organization's growth.

- **12-Month Cash Flow (12-MCF)**

  A financial plan to enhance profits through increasing income and decreasing expenses.

- **Seven-Touch Marketing Plan (7-TMP)**

  A marketing plan to ensure your message will reach your target market.

- **One-Page Action Plan (1-PAP)**

  A roadmap on how to implement your strategic plan.

At this point, you should have an accurate picture of where your business is today, where you want it to be in the future, and exactly what steps you are going to take to move your vision into reality. Remember that this is a process and from time to time we need to take a look at the environment around us. Examine what has changed and what effect that may have on our forward progress. To be highly successful, we must recognize that the tools, techniques, and concepts we have learned about are not engraved in stone, but rather are living documents that must adapt to the surrounding situations.

Use the checklists that follow to review your 1-PSP and 1-PAP to make sure you covered all the bases. Be thoughtful and honest as you look through your documents (1-PRC, 12-MCF, and 7-TMP) and check your plan.

Finally, take a moment to reflect on life balance and what your long-term goals are. Do not be so wrapped up with the present that you lose focus on what is really important to you.

People Checklist

If at any point during the re-examination you need to make adjust-ments, do so immediately. The purpose of this review is to make sure you understand not only what you have done so far, but what is required to make sure your business grows and is successful.

With your 1-PSP, 1-PAP, and 1-PRC in front of you, ask yourself the following:

Y/N	Points to Consider	Comments
	Do I have a strategic objective related to people?	
	If not, do I need one? If yes, consider one now and write it in on the 1-PSP.	
	Are there goals associated with my People objectives?	
	If not, why not? Each Objective needs a Goal to define it.	
	Have I identified tactics for each People goal?	
	Do I have tactics that need to be refined further?	
	Do my goals and tactics follow the S.M.A.R.T. process?	
	Have I identified appropriate measurements for each tactic?	
	Does each tactic have a responsible individual assigned to it?	
	Have I made sure resources are available for a successful completion of each tactic?	

Before we leave the People Strategy, take one last look at it from the perspective of S.T.A.R.

Y/N	Points to Consider	Comments
	Strategize – Have I considered my strengths, opportunities, and dangers?	
	Target – Have I clearly stated what the result will look like?	
	Act – Have I left any steps out that will impact my ability to succeed?	
	Reflect – Have I allowed time to adjust throughout the process if necessary?	

Operations Checklist

Operations are the hub of our business. In a very real sense we need it running like a well-oiled machine. But it does not get there without our attention to maintenance. The 1-PSP and 1-PAP are our maintenance tools and it is up to us to make sure we use them continuously and not to miss opportunities for improvement. At the end of the day, this is our competitive advantage!

With your 1-PSP and 1-PAP in front of you, ask yourself:

Y/N	Points to Consider	Comments
	Do I have a strategic objective related to operations?	
	If not, do I need one? If yes, consider one now and write it in on the 1-PSP.	
	Are there goals associated with my Operations objectives?	
	If not, why not? Each Objective needs a Goal to define it.	
	Have I identified tactics for each Operations goal?	
	Do I have tactics that need to be refined further?	
	Do my goals and tactics follow the S.M.A.R.T. process?	
	Have I identified appropriate measurements for each tactic?	
	Does each tactic have a responsible individual assigned to it?	
	Have I made sure resources are available for a successful completion of each tactic?	

Before we leave the Operations Strategy, take one last look at it from the perspective of S.T.A.R.

Y/N	Points to Consider	Comments
	Strategize – Have I considered my strengths, opportunities, and dangers?	
	Target – Have I clearly stated what the result will look like?	
	Act – Have I left any steps out that will impact my ability to succeed?	
	Reflect – Have I allowed time to adjust throughout the process if necessary?	

Finance Checklist

The financial health of your business is in your hands. As awesome a responsibility as that may be, it is also one that can be extremely exciting and rewarding. This is accomplished when you take control of the finances instead of allowing the finances to control you!

It may be helpful to have available your recent financial statements and your 12-Month Cash Flow plan completed earlier:

Y/N	Points to Consider	Comments
	Do I have a strategic objective related to finance?	
	If not, do I need one? If yes, consider one now and write it in on the 1-PSP.	
	Are there goals associated with my Finance objectives?	
	If not, why not? Each Objective needs a Goal to define it.	
	Have I identified tactics for each Finance goal?	
	Do I have tactics that need to be refined further?	
	Do my goals and tactics follow the S.M.A.R.T. process?	
	Have I identified appropriate measurements for each tactic?	
	Does each tactic have a responsible individual assigned to it?	
	Have I made sure resources are available for a successful completion of each tactic?	

Look again at your Financial S.T.A.R.

Y/N	Points to Consider	Comments
	Strategize – Have I considered my strengths, opportunities, and dangers?	
	Target – Have I clearly stated what the result will look like?	
	Act – Have I left any steps out that will impact my ability to succeed?	
	Reflect – Have I allowed time to adjust throughout the process if necessary?	

Marketing Checklist

Marketing is always an area of the business where we can see rapid results from our efforts. However, it is also an area where we can continue to throw good money after bad. To avoid this scenario, it is imperative that we follow our marketing plan, track the results, and review the progress continuously. Make sure you have captured this concept in your 1-PSP and 1-PAP.

With your 1-PSP, 1-PAP, and 7-TMP in front of you, ask yourself the following:

Y/N	Points to Consider	Comments
	Do I have a strategic objective related to marketing?	
	If not, do I need one? If yes, consider one now and write it in on the 1-PSP.	
	Are there goals associated with my Marketing objectives?	
	If not, why not? Each Objective needs a Goal to define it.	
	Have I identified tactics for each Marketing goal?	
	Do I have tactics that need to be refined further?	
	Do my goals and tactics follow the S.M.A.R.T. process?	
	Have I identified appropriate measurements for each tactic?	
	Does each tactic have a responsible individual assigned to it?	
	Have I made sure resources are available for a successful completion of each tactic?	

Before we leave the Marketing Strategy, take one last look at it from the perspective of S.T.A.R.

Y/N	Points to Consider	Comments
	Strategize – Have I considered my strengths, opportunities, and dangers?	
	Target – Have I clearly stated what the result will look like?	
	Act – Have I left any steps out that will impact my ability to succeed?	
	Reflect – Have I allowed time to adjust throughout the process if necessary?	

Life Balance

What is important in your personal life? What is important to your business? Your life is a journey and it is important to make decisions that will lead you toward your desired destination. You set priorities that indicate what is important to you.

What are your long-term goals? Will going into business assist or prevent you from going where you want to go? Think through all aspects of your life and plan with peace in mind.

Your business goals only define one dimension of your life. The goals you set for each dimension will affect the others, so do not set goals in just one area. Consider what you want to accomplish while considering the impact on all of the areas.

	This Year	Life	Five Years
Spiritual and Emotional			
Physical and Health			
Education			
Family and Friends			
Financial			
Social Community			
Employment			

Create Sustainable Success

Small business strategic planning depends on you, the leader who can successfully transform, innovate, stabilize, and grow your business. A successful strategic planning process is the foundation of creating sustainable success and is controlled by you.

Be inspired!

"A thought, even a possibility, can shatter and transform us"
Friedrich Nietzsche

"Innovation distinguishes between a leader and a follower."
Steve Jobs

"True stability results when presumed order and presumed disorder are balanced. A truly stable system expects the unexpected, is prepared to be disrupted, and waits to be transformed."
Tom Robbins

"If we're growing, we're always going to be out of our comfort zone."
John Maxwell

Believe!

Succeed!

Appendix A: Web Sites for Business

Illinois Small Business Development Center -
wpdi.clcillinois.edu/sbdc/

Naming Your Business:
Illinois -
www.cyberdriveillinois.com/departments/business_services/corp.html
Trademark / Service Mark - www.uspto.gov
    TESS - tess2.uspto.gov/bin/gate.exe?f=tess&state=5970pg.1.1
Domain Name - www.networksolutions.com
Software:
www.paloalto.com
www.intuit.com

Small Business:
www.census.gov
www.score.org
www.askjim.biz
www.smallbusinessadvocate.com
www.sba.gov
office.microsoft.com/en-us/templates/default.aspx
www.tannedfeet.com - Legal information
www.ienconnect.com – Illinois Entrepreneurial Network - State resources
www.irs.gov/businesses/small/index.html
www.bls.gov/OCO

State of Illinois
www.state.il.us/dcfs/index.shtml - Department of Children and Family
Services
www.idfpr.com - Illinois Department of Professional Regulations – licensing
www.revenue.state.il.us - Illinois Department of Revenue

Through local libraries, use Reference USA (InfoUSA) to obtain a list of
competitors in specific geographic areas. The data can also be used to look
for sales leads, find new business opportunities, and track phone numbers
and addresses for public and private companies.

Appendix B: References

"Growing Your Business Through Principled Networking" by Julia Hubbel, published by Ernst & Young LLP.

Jim Blasingame, www.smallbusinessadvocate.com.

Andrea Nierenberg, www.smallbusinessadvocate.com/small-business-braintrust/andrea-nierenberg-377.

Boomer, L. Gary (06/24/05) "Tips for holding a successful accounting firm summit" Microsoft Dynamics,
www.microsoft.com/dynamics/accountingprofessionals/ap_boomer_firmsummit.mspx#EPC.

Mind Tools Ltd, (2009), Using the TOWS Matrix:
www.mindtools.com/pages/article/newSTR_89.htm.

Orme, Denis, (2007), "Your Leading Ways Newsletter",
No. 23: www.leader-success.com/newsletter23.htm.

Payne, Stephen G. (10/10/06), "Driving Growth Through Leadership" Princeton Regional Chamber of Commerce, 2006 Fall Workshop Slide Presentation,
www.leaderx.com/multimedia/PRCC_Growth_Workshop_PreWork.ppt#279,1,Slide 1.

Drucker, Peter F. (1954), "The Practice of Management", New York: New York, HarperCollins Publishers, Inc., 10 East 53rd Street.

Nikitina, Arina (2008), www.goal-setting-guide.com/smart-goals.html, Wikipedia (2008), www.wikipedia.org/wiki/SMART_(project_management).

Wiley Publishing Co. (2009), www.dummies.com/how-to/content/setting-smart-management-goals.html.

Insights - Insights Learning & Development Ltd, Jack Martin Way, Claverhouse Business Park, Dundee DD4 9FF, Scotland, UK,insights@insights.com www.insights.com.

Sargent, D., Sargent, M., Wold, D. P. (September, 2005). "Part VIII: Managing Your Money". NxLeveL® Guide for Entrepreneurs, Fourth Edition. USA:NxLeveL® Education Foundation.

Brigham, E. F., Houston, J. F. (2007), Fundamentals of Financial Managerment, Eleventh Edition. Mason, OH: Thompson South-Western.

Fry, F. L. Ph.D., Stoner, C. R. Ph.D., and Weinzimmer, L. G. Ph.D., (2005). "Running the Numbers", Strategic Planning for Small Business Made Easy. Madison, Wisconsin:CWL Publishing Enterprises, Inc.

Low, Robert (2004), Accounting and Finance for Small Business Made Easy. Madison, Wisconsin: CWL Publishing Enterprises, Inc.

Williams, Jan R.; Susan F. Haka, Mark S. Bettner, Joseph V. Carcello (2008). *Financial & Managerial Accounting*. McGraw-Hill Irwin.

Ward, Susan (2008). "Cash Flow Management"
sbinfocanada.about.com/cs/management/g/cashflowmgt.htm.

Growing Your Business (December 11, 2003). "How To Better Manage Your Cash Flow" Entreprenuer.com,
www.entrepreneur.com/money/moneymanagement/managingcashflow/article66008.html.

Epstein, Barry J.; Eva K. Jermakowicz (2007). Interpretation and Application of International Financial Reporting Standards. John Wiley & Sons. p. 1.

Karen E. Spaeder, "10 Ways to Grow You're Business", May 11, 2004,
www.entrepreneur.com/interstitial/Ent_Interstitial.aspx?URL=/management/growingyourbusiness/article70660.htm.

Andrew Bordeaux, "Marketing Misconceptions", July 23, 2008, Grow Think,
www.growthink.com/content/3-common-marketing-misconceptions.

Graphics from Microsoft, http://office.microsoft.com/en-us/clipart/default.aspx.

Appendix C: Forms

1-PSP (One-Page Strategic Plan)

Marketing

Finance

Operations

People

1-PRC (One-Page Relationship Chart)

Name	Role	Differences	Similarities	Value	Action

12-Month Cash Flow

	Start-up	Month 1	Month 2	Month 3	Month 4	Month 5	Month 6	Month 7	Month 8	Month 9	Month 10	Month 11	Month 12	Year 1 Total
Beg. Cash Receipts														
Loan Equity														
TOTAL CASH														
COGS														
Officer's Salary														
Sub-Contract Labor														
Payroll Taxes														
Rent														
Utilities														
Telephone														
Maintenance														
Insurance														
Advertising														
Office Expense														
Supplies														
Professional Fees														
License														
Bank Charges														
Travel & Entertain														
Furniture & Fixture														
Equipment														
Misc. or 10% Contingency														
TOTAL EXPENSE														
NET CASH OUTLAY														
Loan														
End Cash														

Seven-Touch Marketing Plan (7-TMP)

This report indicates the customers, the methods used to penetrate the market, and the estimated budget necessary to implement the marketing strategy.

	Target Market	Seven-Touch Methods	Frequency	Cost
1.				
2.				
3.				
4.				
5.				
6.				
7.				
		Total Cost		

SMALL BUSINESS STRATEGIC PLANNING

1-PAP (One-Page Action Plan)

Strategy

Objective

Goal

	Completion Date:				
Tactic	Completion Date	Responsibility	Cost	Results	Achieved Yes / No

1-PSP (One-Page Strategic Plan)

Earth Paints Collections

Eliminate the impact of paint disposal in landfills through recycling

	People		Operations		Finance		Marketing	
	EPA	ACE Regional Manager	Location	Product Disposal	COGs	New Product	Acme Hardware	Decals
	Consult with EPA officials by 8/1	Meet with Acme Regional Manager Annually	Find larger facility by 3/1	Define policies for waste product disposal by 5/1	Determine accurate COGs by 12/1	Determine impact of new product by 12/1	Collection process advertised by Acme Nationwide by 8/1	Send letters of introduction with decals by 10/1
	Verify EPA Contact by 6/1	Invite Regional Manager to meet for lunch by 2/1	Calculate space requirements by 11/1	List products that need to be disposed properly by 3/15	Calculate fixed costs by 8/1	Calculate COGs for new product estimate numbers by 10/1	Determine contact by 6/1	Design decal w/ logo By 8/1
	E-mail Questions and concerns by 6/15	Send discussion items and materials by 3/1	Discuss requirements with realtor by 1/1	Calculate value of disposed product by 3/25	Calculate variable costs by 8/15	Negotiate prices by 10/1	Send Letter of introduction by 6/15	Compile list or recipients by 8/15
	Phone contact by 7/1	Follow-up with phone call by 4/1	Visit viable sites by 2/1	List options by 4/1	Prepare Income Statement by 9/1	Create Cash Flow by 11/1	Request referral from Midwest by 7/1	Write letter by 9/1
					Identify potential savings by 10/1		Follow-up via phone by 7/15	Duplicate letter by 9/15
	Open Lines of communication by 8/1	Meeting Scheduled by 4/15	List options by 3/1	Policies Completed by 5/1	COGs by 12/1	New Product Costs by 12/1	Acme Flyer by 8/1	Decals in Letters by 10/1

1-PRC (One-Page Relationship Chart)

Name	Role	Differences	Similarities	Value	Objective
Peter Man	ACE Midwest Manager	Analytical, Careful, precise, detailed	Hard working	Supportive, respected, decision maker	Provide details and information he needs
Susie Song	Paint Company Sales Rep	Outgoing, hard to pin down		Knows everyone in industry	Regularly meet to understand trends
Pat Anderson	Truck Driver		Hard working, competent	Picks up paint to recycle	Reward and complement on job well done
Harmony Smith	Government EPA Staff		Committed to protecting environment	Partner in providing government support	Provide continual updates on business

Earth Paints
12 - Month Cash Flow

	3/1/2009 Month 1	4/1/2009 Month 2	5/1/2009 Month 3	6/1/2009 Month 4	7/1/2009 Month 5	8/1/2009 Month 6	9/1/2009 Month 7	10/1/2009 Month 8	11/1/2009 Month 9	12/1/2009 Month 10	1/1/2010 Month 11	2/1/2010 Month 12	Year 1 TOTAL
Beg. Cash	578,194	867,167	950,854	1,059,698	1,229,661	1,452,666	1,857,098	2,088,171	2,368,843	2,492,331	2,457,121	2,469,693	578,194
Recepts	238,561	269,431	381,098	359,828	414,529	597,832	510,432	474,121	315,211	210,040	201,412	221,009	4,193,504
Loan	250,000												250,000
Equity	125,000												125,000
TOTAL CASH	1,191,755	1,136,598	1,331,952	1,419,526	1,644,190	2,050,498	2,367,530	2,562,292	2,684,054	2,702,371	2,658,533	2,690,702	5,146,698
COGS1	125,348	125,348	125,348	125,348	125,348	125,348	125,348	125,348	125,348	125,348	125,348	125,348	1,504,176
Officer's Salary	4,750	4,750	4,750	4,750	4,750	4,750	4,750	4,750	4,750	4,750	4,750	4,750	57,000
Sub-Contract Labor	10,382	11,420	12,562	13,818	15,200	16,720	18,392	16,553	14,898	13,408	12,067	10,860	166,282
Payroll Taxes	892	981	1,079	1,187	1,306	1,437	1,580	1,422	1,280	1,152	1,037	933	14,287
Rent	2,700	2,700	2,700	2,700	2,700	2,700	2,700	2,700	2,700	2,700	2,700	2,700	32,400
Utilities	1,389	1,458	1,531	1,608	1,688	1,773	1,861	1,768	1,680	1,596	1,516	1,440	19,310
Telephone	183	183	183	183	183	183	183	183	183	183	183	183	2,196
Maintenance	589	592	595	598	601	604	607	610	613	616	619	622	7,266
Insurance	513	513	513	513	513	513	513	513	513	513	513	513	6,156
Advertising	2,759	2,773	2,787	2,801	2,815	2,829	2,843	2,857	2,871	2,886	2,900	2,915	34,034
Office Expense	359	200	275	321	281	290	211	238	231	345	321	231	3,303
Supplies	298	299	301	302	304	306	307	309	310	312	313	315	3,676
Professional Fees	2,035	2,098	2,159	2,224	2,290	2,359	2,430	2,503	2,578	2,655	2,735	2,817	28,881
License	135	135	135	135	135	135	135	135	135	135	135	135	1,620
Bank Charges	109	110	110	111	101	102	102	117	143	112	113	121	1,349
Travel & Entertain.	1,287	1,326	1,365	1,406	1,449	1,492	1,537	1,583	1,630	1,679	1,730	1,782	18,265
Furniture & Fixture	0	0	0	0	0	0	0	0	0	0	0	0	0
Equipment	125000		75,000				75000			50000			325,000
Misc. or 10% contingency	30,000	15,000	25,000	16,000	16,000	16,000	25,000	16,000	16,000	21,000	18,000	16,000	228,000
TOTAL EXPENSE	308,728	169,884	256,394	174,005	175,664	177,539	263,499	177,589	175,863	229,390	172,980	171,665	2,453,201
NET CASH OUTLAY	883,027	966,714	1,075,558	1,245,521	1,468,526	1,872,958	2,104,031	2,384,703	2,508,191	2,472,981	2,485,553	2,519,037	2,693,497
Loan	15,860	15,860	15,860	15,860	15,860	15,860	15,860	15,860	15,860	15,860	15,860	15,860	190,320
END CASH	867,167	950,854	1,059,698	1,229,661	1,452,666	1,857,098	2,088,171	2,368,843	2,492,331	2,457,121	2,469,693	2,503,177	2,503,177

Seven-Touch Marketing Plan (7-TMP)

This report indicates the customers, the methods used to penetrate the market, and the estimated budget necessary to implement the marketing strategy.

	Method	Description	Frequency	Cost
1	Letter w/ decal	Send letter to all Acme Hardware Managers with recycle decal	1	$150
2	Personal Visit	Visit Midwest locations and introduce Earth Paint Collections to manager.	1	$0
3	Brochure	Leave brochure with Business card and contact information	1	$250
4	Press Release	E-Mail new product information and latest government regulations to 100 newspapers	3	$0
5	Radio Interview	Present environment concerns for land fill, toxic waste, and water contamination. Offer solution for paint recycling.	1	$0
6	e-Mail	Collect E-mails of potential Paint Collection Sites and provide updates on new laws and issues impacting recycling paint	1	$0
7	Phone call	Follow-up calls to all managers visited to answer questions on paint recycling	1	$0
			Total Cost	$300

1-PAP (One-Page Action Plan)

Strategy	Marketing						
Objective	Acme Hardware				Completion Date:		
Goal	Tactic	Date	Responsibility	Cost	Results	Achieved Yes / No	
Collection process advertised Nationally by September 1	Determine contact pointy	3/1	George	$0	Name to Contact	Yes	
	Send letter of introduction	3/15	George	$0	Introduction Letter sent	Yes	
	Request referral	4/1	George	$0	Contact Midwest Manager	No	
	Support Acme Promotional Campaign	9/1	George	$0	Advertisement in Circular	No	

About the Authors

Claudia Pannell is a business and financial coach with the Pannell Advisory Group, Inc. In this capacity she helps clients address today's business and financial challenges. Clients seeking assistance come from small, medium and large businesses and include individual owners to Fortune 500 management teams.

Prior to launching the Pannell Advisory Group, Inc., Claudia contracted for The Vision Tree, Ltd., and spent 15 years at Abbott in Dallas, Texas and Lake County, Illinois. While at Abbott, she served as a Computer Analyst, Project Leader, and Systems Manager. Additionally, she served as a corporate mentor and Officer of the IT Women's Leadership Network. During her time at Abbott, she successfully honed her leadership skills and served as a facilitator for strategic planning sessions.

Claudia offers her clients a wide range of programs and services including workshops for teambuilding, problem solving, innovation, change management and strategic planning. Most activities are designed for clients to identify the problem areas of their organization, analyze potential solutions and develop manageable action plans that can be implemented to improve the situation.

Her book *Strategic Planning for Project Management* was published in 2009 and is designed to assist individuals seeking certification in project management by the Project Management Institute. Additionally, she has co-authored, the *Strategic Planning Workbook Creating Sustainable Success* also published in 2009. This workbook is the text for our 16-hour workshop which focuses its participants on building a strategic plan and implementing it.

To contact Claudia Pannell, e-Mail her at Claudia@VisionTreeForums.com.

Joanne Osmond is a reformer and change agent. She is recognized for transforming both individuals and organizations. While at Abbott Laboratories, Joanne received an international award, the 2000 Help Desk Institute's Team Excellence Award for operational excellence by developing the right organization, processes, and technology to provide consistent delivery of customer support. In 2003, she received the ATHENA Award for assisting women in reaching their full leadership potential while demonstrating excellence, creativity, and initiative in her profession.

As the owner and President of Market Drafters, Joanne works with the Small Business Development Center in assisting entrepreneurs to move to the next level. Market Drafters provides individuals, small businesses, and not-for-profit organizations with Web hosting and design. To create sustainable success, she partners with her clients to drive search engine optimization and self-management of the site by the owner. The books she has authored and published cover business planning, Scouting in the LDS Church, and a collection of stories about her daughter who has Down's syndrome. She is the recipient of the Boy Scout's Silver Beaver Award and serves on the Council's Executive Board as the Vice President of Membership. She has served on the Lake Villa Elementary School Board for 18 years, elected to serve her sixteenth year on Lake's Division of the IASB currently serving as the Director representing Lake County on the state association board. In addition, Joanne serves on the Special Education of Lake County Executive Board.

To contact Joanne Osmond, e-Mail her at Jo@VisionTreeForums.com.

Vision Tree Forums

Claudia and Joanne combine their expertise and commitment to entrepreneurs to bring online training, forums, and workshops to the small business community. Focused on helping owners plan for success, Vision Tree Forums presents a wide selection of options for learning.

Solutions include both online training and in-person workshops coupled with an accountability partnership that strengthens the participants and ensures success. Whether considering opening your doors or reevaluating a long standing business, Vision Tree Forums provides solutions and assistance in meeting specific small business needs.

Claudia's expertise in project management and managing business finances plus her affiliation with Dave Ramsey's philosophy of money management provides a firm foundation to support growing businesses in diverse fields.

Joanne's background in customer service, marketing, and information technology provides a perfect balance to Claudia providing participants with a full circle of support as they start or expand their small business.

Online Training is provided at www.SmallBusinessSpokenHere.com. Available forums include:

Are You Ready? – This online forum explores your options and readiness to start your own business. It assists in setting goals to be prepared when you do decide to venture out as an entrepreneur.

Starting a Business – This online forum was developed and provided to the Small Business Development Center located at the College of Lake County, Illinois. Basics for starting a business are similar in all states and would apply to anyone who is starting a business. This is a two hour overview of all of the components required to start a business.

The Simple Business Plan – This online forum breaks the business plan into simple steps and walks the participant through developing a business plan that will be a road map for starting the business and in most cases can be submitted for financing.

Strategic Planning for Small Business – The forum is best implemented with an in-person component and an accountability partner assigned to provide initial support and reporting. The objective of the forum is to create a one-page strategic plan that becomes a platform to develop a detailed action plan.

Get Ready! Get Set! Grow! – This series of online forums allows a new business owner to select specific areas where assistance may be needed when starting or building a small business. Guest speakers address business organizations, accounting, marketing, and other areas of expertise required to run a successful small business.

For more information: www.visiontreeforums.com.

Contact us for speaking engagements at info@visiontreeforums.com, 847 265 9433.